YEAR GROUP
PHOTOCOPIABLES

YEAR

Paul and Jean Noble

CREDITS

Authors
Paul and Jean Noble

Editor
David Sandford

Assistant Editor
Christine Harvey

Series designer
Lynne Joesbury

Designer
Paul Cheshire

Illustrations
Ray and Corrine Burrows (pages 110–22, 126–7, 130–1, 135, 160–7)
Peter Smith (pages 5–109, 122–5, 128, 132–4, 136–59, 168–76)
Neil Gower (page 118 top)

Cover photographs
Manipulated images © Photodisc (globe, dice, magnet, paintbrush, disk);
© Digital Vision (hand); © Stockbyte (mask)

Published by Scholastic Ltd,
Villiers House,
Clarendon Avenue,
Leamington Spa,
Warwickshire
CV32 5PR
Printed by Bell & Bain Ltd, Glasgow
Text © 2002 Paul and Jean Noble
© 2002 Scholastic Ltd
3 4 5 6 7 8 9 0   4 5 6 7 8 9 0 1

Visit our website at www.scholastic.co.uk

British Library Cataloguing-in-Publication Data
A catalogue record for this book is available from
the British Library.

ISBN 0-439-01989-3

CONTENTS

INTRODUCTION

Teaching Year 2

Teaching top infants can be a particular joy, certainly in our experience. Children of this age have acquired a degree of confidence and independence that encourages the giving of responsibility. Especially in infant schools, where they are clearly top dogs, Year 2 children are often given useful and valuable administrative and social tasks to carry out. They are also more socially aware and intellectually focused than younger infants, and this gives them a responsiveness that can be very rewarding to the teacher. It is generally true that, although teachers are conscious of the pressure of SATs – and of the force that it brings to bear on the curriculum – the children are not, which makes Year 2 a lively and satisfying age group to teach.

Children face the whole range of curriculum subjects, as they did in Year 1, but there is a growing tendency for the content of subjects to 'harden up' and to be more precisely defined. For example, it is likely that in both geography and history, subject matter will be recognisably discipline-specific, with children studying topics such as St Lucia or Guy Fawkes. This begins to make the construction of supportive material, such as these worksheets, a little more problematic, as where choices can be made it is obvious that not everyone will choose to do the same thing. Learning, however (particularly within the Literacy and Numeracy Strategies), is laid down in considerable detail, and elsewhere we have been able to lean heavily upon the schemes of work drawn up by the Qualifications and Curriculum Authority; schemes that are widely used as the basis for school syllabuses. (Refer to www.qca.org.uk or www.standards.dfee.gov.uk schemes.)

The *Year Group Photocopiables* series draws on substantial teaching experience and can provide accessible, easy-to-use support for teachers under the pressure of time in the classroom, or help to meet the needs of voracious learners. Supply teachers and others 'caught on the hop' will also be able to rely on this material to help them to cope with demanding days.

You will hardly need reminding that, although these worksheets can support your teaching, they cannot do it for you. A whole school full of overheated photocopiers will not make children learn; it is for you to capture their interest, and stimulate and provide for the mental and physical activity that needs to accompany learning at this stage.

What the photocopiable sheets cover

This particular volume is based upon the range of curriculum topics described in *The National Curriculum: Handbook for primary teachers in England* (www.nc.uk.net), and the worksheets have been compiled bearing in mind the demands of the Literacy and Numeracy Strategies, as well as QCA subject guidance. Inevitably, weighting has been given to the core subjects (English, mathematics and science), but the non-core foundation subjects (with the exception of PE) are included to varying degrees, depending upon the suitability of the content to the photocopiable format. Non-foundation subjects (such as RE, PSHE and even citizenship) are covered where subject matter allows.

Of course, these worksheets cannot deal with everything laid down in the curriculum, nor with everything in your school syllabus, so cannot constitute a complete curriculum. But they do aim to give essential support for the core of your teaching: rather like basic car insurance, the cover provided here is fundamental rather than comprehensive. A book that attempted to be comprehensive would be many times larger than this, as well as being difficult to justify in principle – nobody would want infant children to overdose on worksheets.

The choice of content was made on the following grounds:
● Content and activities must translate sensibly to the photocopiable format (activities that are predominantly 'hands-on', colour dependent or oral have largely been avoided)
● Activities must be worthwhile and interesting
● Subject matter should relate directly to the National Curriculum.
● Content should satisfy the demands of the Literacy and Numeracy Strategies where possible.
Children at Year 2 require teaching that includes a great deal of practice and repetition, but we have largely avoided providing repetitious sheets in favour of range of cover and in order to keep the book to a manageable size. However, suggestions for reinforcement and extension are included in the teachers' notes.

Using the material

Before you use any sheet it is recommended that you read the teachers' notes that accompany it. These have deliberately been kept brief, but they each contain four sections:

Objective

This states the teaching objective. Each objective is linked to the curriculum guidance issued by the government – in numeracy and literacy, for example, the objectives match targets specified in the Numeracy and Literacy Strategies. Objectives have been stated in direct and non-pretentious terms. However, it is not claimed that children completing a particular sheet will therefore fully achieve that objective – we wish that teaching and learning were that easy!

What to do

Suggestions on how to use each worksheet repeatedly refer to the adult support that children will require and to the importance of talk and discussion. It is very important to get children to 'think out loud' as an aid to learning, but we have also made the assumption that Year 2 children will not, by and large, have reached a high level of reading competence, and we expect that they will be given oral instruction and support. Instructions given on the sheets are kept as brief as possible, sometimes serving as memory jogger to the teacher rather than as instructions to the child. The teachers' notes state when and what equipment will be required (usually very little), how the activity might be taught (through whole-class, group or individual instruction, for example), and the degree of adult support that is likely to be needed.

Differentiation

This is a big word that covers some very simple strategies. Sometimes, all that is needed to give access to a particular activity for all the children in a group is differentiation by the extent of the attention and instruction given. The more able will be able to proceed with the minimum of instruction; the less able may need adult support throughout. It is rarely the case that an entirely different activity will be needed to differentiate in order to meet an objective, but where appropriate you will find suggestions in the teachers' notes.

Extension

Extension activities can be used as a form of differentiation for the more able children, but they are mainly intended to provide some form of reinforcement to help the objective to be achieved. Unless particular apparatus or teaching is required, most extension activities could be completed at home. It is recommended that careful consideration of the issues – including support provided for parents, the value of the work at home, and competing demands on a child's time – be undertaken before sheets are issued as homework. Teachers seeking further extension work, or more differentiation for the able child, should consult companion volumes in this series.

Progression

The order of the sheets has been kept as logical as possible, but the order will not necessarily match the order of your teaching programme, and in some subject areas there is simply no obvious order for the teaching of particular material. Nevertheless, a thread of progression runs through the book and, more visibly, through the series. This is inevitable as the material is tied to a progressive curriculum, and this provides the added bonus that reference can be made, both forwards and backwards, for more, or less, challenging activities for children to undertake.

ENGLISH

The National Literacy Strategy is pretty demanding in Year 2. This is partly due to the fact that it requires repetition of material covered in previous years, but also because it tries to build up a child's knowledge of English brick by brick. Of course, our acquisition of language does not quite work in this way – we are not taught every single digraph and phoneme. In this section, we have tried to avoid travelling over ground covered by previous volumes in this series, and we have also acknowledged that, in a wide-ranging book such as this, we cannot cover everything.

We have concentrated on what lends itself most readily to the worksheet format, so you will find a distinct bias towards word-level work and considerably less emphasis on text-level work, where comprehension and composition really demand the kind of stimulus and experience not readily compressed into a single sheet of A4. Perhaps more importantly, text-level work can also benefit greatly from adult intervention and social interaction.

As reading skills develop, there are increasing opportunities for children to work on their own, and many of the following sheets can be used for independent work. You may well find that you wish for more practice in a particular area of learning; hopefully, some of the sheets will give you ideas and formats that you can use to produce extra material in a similar form, where needed. For example, it would be easy to use a sheet like Dreamtime (page 32) several times, simply by blanking out the completing phrases, and either leaving blanks for the more able to complete on their own or substituting alternative endings.

For further details of the Literacy Strategy teaching programme, apart from *The National Curriculum* and the *National Literacy Strategy* itself, consult other relevant government publications, in particular those published by the Standards and Effectiveness Unit, for example *The NLS Word Level Work, Activity Resource Bank, Module 2*, published jointly by DfES and OUP.

Hook a word (page 14)

Objective: To teach common spelling patterns for the vowel phoneme *oo* (short as in wood).

What to do: Point out the *oo* sound held in the bird's beak on the worksheet. Recite the rhyme and make sure that the children understand and can recognise the sound. Using the letters held by Captain Hook, ask the children to make as many *oo* words as they can and write them in the space on the right of the sheet (cook, hook, shook, took, nook, look, book).

Differentiation: Less confident children could use a

'try sheet' on which to record attempts at making words. The greatest difficulty children are likely to experience is that of hearing the sound correctly, support for which will require the presence of an adult.

Extension: Challenge children to create other families of rhyming words with the same common phoneme – try -*d* endings (wood, good, hood). There are also the *u* words (pull, hull) to rhyme. Watch out for regional pronunciation variations.

Word shop (page 15)

Objective: To teach common spelling patterns for the phoneme *ar*.

What to do: This is a variation on the last activity, looking this time at the *ar* phoneme. Ask the children to choose a start letter from the list on the left of the sheet and, if this does not make a word, an end letter from the right shelf, to make a proper word. They should write their words in the spaces on the shopping list (car, tar, star, bar, cart, tarn, tart, dart, darn, start, bard, barn, lard). It is also possible to make nonsense words, which you might like to discuss with the children.

Differentiation: As with all phoneme activities, less confident children could use a 'try sheet' to write down attempts at making words. Hearing the sound correctly may again be a problem, and adult support will be needed.

Extension: Children must be able to recognise phonemes in writing as well as speech, so ask them to search for *ar* words in their reading book and make a list of any they find.

Long and short (page 16)

Objective: To discriminate between long and short versions of the *oo* vowel phoneme.

What to do: Explain the difference between long and short phonemes (for example, good and moon) to the children. Read the words in the balloons on the sheet out loud together, then ask the children to colour in the short sound balloons. Once they've coloured the words in, ask the children to copy them into the correct list.

Differentiation: Children who are more able could use two colours, one for long and one for short phonemes. Recite the words with less confident children to help them identify the sounds. Put them in the context of a sentence, and see if they can spot the word and say whether the *oo* sound is long or short. You may, of course, exaggerate for effect.

Extension: Provide further oral practice. Read a prepared passage that includes such *oo* words – remember the *ew* (blew), *ue* (blue) and *u–e* (dune) sounds. Ask the children to raise a hand when they hear the long *oo* sound.

Top-up with oil (page 17)

Objective: To discriminate, spell and read common spelling patterns for the *oy* phoneme (*oi* as in boil).

What to do: Make sure that the children can identify *oy* sounds in words clearly by reciting some examples together. Then, selecting letters from the worksheet, the children add 'oil' to make as many words as possible and write them on the list. Point out to the children that not all the combinations of letters will make real words – what nonsense words can they make?

Differentiation: Give oral support to the less able; the more able could be asked to generate further words from their list (for example, boil may produce boiled, boiling, boiler, boils). These can be written or spoken, according to the ability of the child.

Extension: Ask the children to write and/or say sentences that include each word on their list.

Ship ahoy! (page 18)

Objective: To discriminate, spell and read common spelling patterns for the vowel phoneme *oy* (as in boy).

What to do: The children should already be familiar with the *oy* sound from the previous activity. Now ask them to match it to a different spelling, generating words from the letters on the ship's wheel and writing them on the list.

Differentiation: Provide oral support for less confident children. The more able could generate longer words from their list (for example, toy could produce toying, toys, toyed). These can be written or spoken according to the ability of the child.

Extension: Ask the children to write and/or say sentences that include the words on their list.

Ow! (page 19)

Objective: To discriminate, spell and read common spelling patterns for the vowel phoneme *ow* (as in cow).

What to do: The children should recite 'how now brown cow' as a class, listening to the sounds as they read the words. Using the picture clues on the sheet, ask the children to fill in the blanks to make *ow* words, pointing out that each dash stands for a letter.

Differentiation: This sheet should be easy enough for most children, but additional listening practice (say sentences containing *ow* phonemes, for example 'The cow jumped over the moon making a sound like a hound', or ' "Ow, I've fallen down" said the cow') during which children have to raise a hand every time they hear the sound, is worthwhile. More able children could try and think of other words that contain *ow* sounds.

Extension: Can the children explain what each word means? Ask them to write and/or say sentences including each word on their list.

Make and say (page 20)

Objective: To discriminate, spell and read common spelling patterns for the vowel phoneme *ou* (as in abound).

What to do: Make sure that the children can hear and recognise the *ou* phoneme first, by reading some sentences out loud to the class. Show the children the worksheet, and explain how they should 'top and tail' the *ou* sound in order to make new words to write on the list.

Differentiation: As with all the sheets on vowel phonemes, differentiation will generally involve supporting children who have difficulty discriminating the sounds orally (see earlier activities for ideas).

Extension: Ask children to say and write more *ou* words created from the word list they have made (loud, loudly, louder and so on).

Picture links (1) (page 21)

Objective: To discriminate, spell and read common spelling patterns for the vowel phoneme oo (short, as in foot).

What to do: Each of the four 'Picture links' worksheets works in the same way. Before the activity, the children should recognise the phoneme sound represented by the picture in the middle of the page (remember that there will be regional variation). Go through the sheet and name each object with the children. Tell them that if it contains a sound that matches with the sound in the middle, they should draw a line to link the object with the main picture. You could, of course, vary the child's response: the pictures could be coloured, or put in coloured frames, to indicate the link. Pictures with the same main sound (short oo or u) are: book, wool, hook, bull, crook, pull. You might like to talk to the children about words that sound the same but are spelt differently (such as wool and bull).

Differentiation: Some children may need help in identifying the significant object in the picture (knitting needles instead of wool, for example). Adult support should direct the child to explore the picture and come up with alternative words. Do not dismiss reasonable answers as wrong, simply look for words containing the phoneme.

Extension: On a card or paper strip, ask children to list as many oo words as they can, starting with the words on the worksheet. They could go on to generate more words from those on the list: pull, pulled, pulling and so on.

Picture links (2) (page 22)

Objective: To discriminate, spell and read common spelling patterns for the vowel phoneme ar (as in far).

What to do: The 'Picture links' worksheets should each be treated in the same way. See the notes for 'Picture links (1)'. The ar words are: arm, tart, car, shark.

Differentiation/Extension: Follow the approach outlined in 'Picture links (1)'.

Picture links (3) (page 23)

Objective: To discriminate, spell and read common spelling patterns for the vowel phoneme oy (as in ploy and boil), including different spellings of the same sound.

What to do: The 'Picture links' worksheets should each be treated in the same way. See the notes for 'Picture links (1)'. The oy words are: toy, soil, coil, boil.

Differentiation/Extension: Follow the approach outlined in 'Picture links (1)'.

Say and sort (1, 2 and 3)
(pages 24–26)

Objective: To identify the three vowel phonemes air, or and er.

What to do: These three worksheets can be mounted on card, cut out and used for sorting sound families. Before sorting, recite the vowel phonemes on the cards with the children so they are familiar with the sounds, then ask the children to sort the cards into families based on the vowel phonemes they have identified. Two or three children might play a game with the cards. Place the cards face-down in a pile. Each child takes a card in turn, says the word and places the card into one of three piles according to the vowel phoneme.

Differentiation: More able children should identify the words and make written lists of each phoneme. The less able may need help identifying the pictures (rabbit or hare, for example). Make it clear that each picture must belong to one of the categories of sound.

Extension: The National Literacy Strategy requires children to identify these phonemes both in speech and in writing, and to recognise common spelling patterns. Extension should therefore move into using the written words themselves. Write the corresponding word on the back of each card, and use them in the same way as before (if you play the game, leave the cards word-side upwards). Less able children can always refer to the pictures on the reverse if they have difficulty.

Answers: The three groups are: bear, stairs, hair, fair, hare, chair, pear, square, tear (as in 'rend'); stork, fork, chalk, paw, claw, cork, core, sword, torch; fur, bird, kerb, shirt, girl, skirt, church, nurse, and purse.

Odd word out (page 27)

Objective: To identify the vowel phoneme air.

What to do: Encourage the children to read each row of words on the worksheet and, after recognising the phoneme common to three of the words, to colour the odd word out in each group. You might like to point out how, even though the sounds are the same, the phonemes are sometimes spelt differently. The odd ones out on the sheet are: more, bird, desk, torn, were and turn.

Differentiation: Where children have a problem reading the words, provide adult support. The exercise can then be completed as described above. More able children might write down groups of words of their own containing a specified phoneme, and an 'odd one out' for a friend to identify.

Extension: A similar exercise can be constructed focusing on the vowel phonemes *or* and *er*. This can be done by blanking the words out on a copy of the worksheet and substituting new ones.

A necklace of rhymes (page 28)

Objective: To discriminate, spell and read the phonemes *ear* (hear) and *ea* (head).

What to do: Explain the sheet to the children. Make sure they know what they should be listening for as they read the words around the necklace. After reading the words, tell them to colour the beads as instructed on the sheet: *Colour the fear rhymes blue and the dead rhymes red.*

Differentiation: Differentiate through the amount of oral support given to the children. Some will need the words read for them.

Extension: Ask the children to design jewel extensions for the necklace, writing *ear* and *ea* words of their own (including variations of words already there, such as 'fearful'). Words not containing either phoneme could be coloured another colour to complete a pretty necklace.

I went to town... (page 29)

Objective: To develop awareness of words that link sentences.

What to do: Children should read the speech bubbles on the worksheet, completing each sentence by adding an appropriate phrase to the sentence stem, based on one of the ideas listed on the right, that fits with the link word and makes sense. For example, 'I went to town until three o'clock'. Point out the idea bubbles on the right for ideas to complete their sentences, and explain that there are more ideas than speech bubbles, and so a number of possible answers.

Differentiation: Talk through the exercise with less able children. Write their suggestions on the board before they complete the exercise by choosing the appropriate phrase from the board to copy onto the sheet.

Extension: See if the children can make up their own 'I went to town...' sentences using the same link words

but completing the sentences differently, for example 'I went to town *until* the park closed'.

Joined-up thinking (page 30)

Objective: To use the language of time to structure a sequence of events.

What to do: This sheet presents the children with a range of sentence stems and, in the balloons, a selection of phrases with which to complete the sentences. Each is linked by a time sequencing word. The children need to decide which two phrases can be linked to make a proper sentence, and then write the completed sentences underneath on the lines provided.

Differentiation: Help those who have difficulty reading the phrases. If the writing proves to be too much of a chore for some, allow them to use a line to link the speech bubble to the balloon.

Extension: Make sure that the time words (after, then, during, before) are clearly identified, then challenge the children to make up their own sentences containing a time-link word, for example 'I was ill *after* eating the hot dog'.

Story starts (page 31)

Objective: To develop story settings by using the strategies of imitation and substitution.

What to do: Explain to the children that these sentences are possible beginnings of stories. Ask: *Can you complete the first sentence?* Share some of the children's ideas for possible sentences before asking them to complete the sentences on the sheet. Make sure they understand that each sentence is the start of a separate story and a new beginning.

Differentiation: The less able could work in a group, with adult support, to make up possible sentence beginnings. Try and make it a fun exercise, even if some of the solutions are a bit silly: 'Suddenly the Queen appeared from underneath the TV!'

Extension: Use the space at the bottom of the sheet for the children to write the beginning of their own story. They could use the sentences as models and write a proper start to a story, although it does not have to be completed. These could be read out to the class, and the rest of the class could finish the story (orally). Who can make the best story?

Dreamtime (page 32)

Objective: To use awareness of grammar to predict from text, and to use the language of time to structure events.

What to do: Together, read the 'dream balloons' on the worksheet, and look at the action cartoons on the bottom of the page to make sure that the children can identify each picture. Explain that they should mix and match the sentence starters and endings to make sentences based on contextual and other clues. The sentences should be completed inside the dream balloons.

Differentiation: In order to help poorer readers, use adult support, or ask groups of children to tackle the problem and to help each other. For less confident writers, the sentences could be linked using a line rather than copying each sentence by hand. More able children could try and complete their own sentences based on the same starters.

Extension: Challenge children to repeat the exercise using their own ideas. This might make a suitable task for completion at home.

What happened yesterday?
(page 33)

Objective: To develop an awareness of past tense.

What to do: This sheet is largely self-explanatory, and should be completed following literacy work on the past tense. You might want to ask the children to indicate their answer by underlining or circling the word, or by writing the entire sentence underneath.

Differentiation: Poor readers will need adult help with reading the sentences on the sheet. However, you will also need to identify children who are unable to discriminate between present and past tense. Before they can complete the sheet successfully, these children need to have plenty of oral practice at making the distinction between past and present tense.

Reinforce the correct, rather than the incorrect, word by discussing events that happened in school 'yesterday' with the children. Make this a regular pastime for a few days.

Extension: Ask the children to write three sentences describing what they did yesterday, in the same format as the sentences on the worksheet.

Mix and make families of words
(page 34)

Objective: To extend vocabulary by building families of words.

What to do: Point out to the children that the three 'root' words on the worksheet are *night, hand* and *day.* Talk about other words that start or end with these words. Ask the children, using the component parts listed, to make as many words as they can for each of the 'root' words, writing them down in the relevant space on the sheet. A dash indicates whether the word part comes before or after the root word.

Differentiation: Make sure that less confident children have a 'try sheet' on which to practice their ideas. Those who are more able might also use a simple dictionary to help them find other words based on the roots on the sheet.

Extension: Ask children to make similar compound word collections of their own as a homework activity. Give them a root word (such as space or post) and see how many words they can come up with.

Shopping lists (page 35)

Objective: To use commas to separate the items in a list.

What to do: Look together at the first list on the worksheet with the children, and talk about how a comma is used to separate each item, but not before the final 'and' in the list. Ask the children to read the three unfinished sentences on the sheet, completing each with a list compiled from the words underneath. Once they have completed the list, they can go on to write their own list on the back of the sheet. There is no limit to its length, except, of course, the size of the page.

Differentiation: Some children may need to practise writing a comma as they may not have done so before. Start large, then get them to practise writing to scale on lined paper. Point out how commas are used in text to help us make sense when we are reading. Play a memory game such as 'I went to market and bought…' in a circle, with an adult scribing the list on a board out of sight of the group. Point out how, in the game, there is always a brief pause where the comma would go in a written list, then show the children the list with commas in to support this.

Extension: Supply a variation of the sheet as homework, asking children to make other lists, such as 'I went on a picnic and took...', 'On holiday I took...', or 'In my school bag there is...'

Comma connections (page 36)

Objective: To look at how commas are used to make connections in sentences.

What to do: The children should join the two parts of each sentence on the sheet, then write out the complete sentence using a comma where the two phrases join.

Differentiation: The more able may write out the complete sentences for themselves, making the connections as instructed. For the less able, it may help to cut out the two parts of each sentence so that they can physically join the parts and see more clearly what the sentence is and how it is connected. Don't make this exercise too fiddly; enlarge the sheet and stick on to card if necessary.

Extension: Ask children to identify sentences in their reading books that contain joining commas. You could ask them to write out a few for homework.

Asking questions: What? Where? When? Who? (page 37)

Objective: To turn statements into questions using a range of *wh* words.

What to do: Show the children the worksheet, and talk about the first completed example on the page. Explain that they should look at the answers on the page and try to think of the question that would produce the answer, using the starter words suggested. Make sure the children are familiar with writing and using question marks.

Differentiation: A group of less able children might do this exercise orally, with an adult as group leader. You might make the sheet into a transparency for an OHP and do the exercise as a class: *Adam went to school. Where?* and so on.

Extension: You can, of course, reverse the process – supplying children with a set of questions and asking them to come up with the answers – but they really need most practice using the *wh* words. Supply some more statements and ask for suitable questions, but don't provide the required *wh* word as a clue.

Sorting syllables (1) and (2)

(pages 38 and 39)

Objective: To discriminate syllables in words orally.

What to do: The two 'Sorting syllables' worksheets are best used together. Cut out the picture cards on both pages and mount them on card. The basic

exercise is to read the word on the card (aided by the picture), then tap out the number of syllables on the desk before sorting the words into sets of one-, two- and three-syllable words. (Don't become too hung up on where the dividing line between syllables is drawn – there are competing conventions covering this issue. Whichever convention is used, the number of syllables is not changed and, in any case, this is primarily an oral exercise for children, not a visual or written one.)

Differentiation: Children will need lots of practice at tapping out syllables. Daily games involving tapping out names are a good way of reinforcing this: 'The monitor today is [point]... Jon–a–than.' An adult could read the words to the children, who should then clap out the syllables.

Extension: Challenge children to find a new word to add to each set. They could draw their own picture cards to go with their words.

At the party (page 40)

Objective: To recognise a variety of forms of questions and to use question marks.

What to do: Ask the children what they think is going on at this party. Read the speech bubbles and eavesdrop on what is happening. Point out that some of the sentences in the speech bubbles are questions – can the children identify which ones? When they have decided, ask the children to add question marks to the end of the questions, and to colour in the balloons that contain the questions.

To help children understand what is happening, allow them to work with a group, with each child pretending to be one of the guests at the party. Discuss what would be the best way to say each line, then ask the children to say their line with the correct intonation. In this way you can tease out the questions, and children could even try to make up suitable responses.

Differentiation: With a less competent group you might read out each balloon in turn (with feeling!), and get children to raise their hands when a question is asked. How can they tell? How can we tell when we only have the words written down?

Extension: Ask children to draw another party scene (or perhaps a classroom one) with lots of large speech bubbles. They can add as much speech as they like, but make sure there are three questions, written correctly using question marks.

Making sense (page 41)

Objective: Using a simple sentence structure as a model, to select words with care, and make new meanings by substitution.

What to do: Read the first, complete, sentence in each section with the children, then ask them to substitute new words in the spaces underneath, creating new sentences with different meanings.

Differentiation: Prepare a list of suitable words for less able children to choose from. You could also talk through their ideas with them before they complete the sheet.

Extension: Talk with the children about the different types of words that can be used to fill the gaps. Ask them to write down six verbs that could complete the sentence 'Josh is...' and six that could complete the sentence 'They are...' Make sure the children are aware of the need for agreement between the verb and nouns/pronouns by modelling a number of examples using variations of the sentences given on the sheet.

Yesterday, in the pond (page 42)

Objective: To develop awareness of the need for grammatical agreement in speech and writing – matching verbs to nouns/pronouns correctly.

What to do: Children should read the story on the worksheet and, as they come to a choice of words, choose the one that agrees with the noun, pronoun or verb in the sentence by underlining or circling their choice.

Differentiation: The most important word in the passage is the first: 'yesterday'. You will need to support less able children by emphasising the fact that everything took place in the past, reiterating this as they tackle each sentence. This may require adult support given most economically to a group of children. More able children could try extending the story by writing further sentences of their own.

Extension: The best way to reinforce this learning is in context rather than in isolated exercises. Ask children to write a few sentences about what they did yesterday, starting the first sentence with 'yesterday' and making sure that all their sentences agree gramatically.

Mandy's muddled messages
(page 43)

Objective: To write clear sentences, using full-stops and capital letters correctly.

What to do: This activity requires children to do more than use correct order and punctuation; they need initially to make sense of all sorts of clues as they read to understand the jumbled words. Explain that these are mobile phone text messages (show them a real one if you can) that have become jumbled. Ask the children to read the words, sort them into a sensible order, then write the sentences on the lines provided.

Differentiation: Those requiring more help could be taught in a group. Draw their attention to the punctuation clues: how does every sentence start? What comes at the end of a sentence? Read the words to the children if they have trouble understanding the sheet.

Extension: Children could compose their own muddled messages and then swap with a friend to see if they can unravel the puzzle. You might like to write a muddled instruction on the board every morning as a challenge for the children to solve.

Angry Andy (page 44)

Objective: To write a simple description and character profile based on simple information.

What to do: Look at the worksheet with the children. What sort of person do they think Andy is? (He's a builder.) Discuss this with the children and examine the clues in the text and the pictures at the top of the page. Then ask the children to write a few sentences about Andy in the space on the worksheet, and to draw a portrait to accompany the text. Encourage them to think about which tells them most about Andy, the words or the picture?

Differentiation: This work can be differentiated through expectation and outcome. As well as simple facts like 'Andy drives a van. Andy is a builder', the more able should be encouraged to write about Andy's character, for example 'Andy eats too much and is rather fat. He gets cross quickly.'

Extension: Children could write a short character sketch of a friend, or find a description from a book to read to the class (perhaps a favourite character).

'Wh'–'ch'–'ph' (page 45)

Objective: To read and spell words containing the digraphs wh, ch and ph.

What to do: Look at the sheet together. Explain that the children should choose the correct digraph from the three at the top of the page to fill the blanks and create a word that describes the picture.

Differentiation: The exercise can be simplified by restricting the digraphs from three to two or even one – simply blank out the words not required. More able children could work with more digraphs on an adapted copy of the worksheet.

Extension: Set the children the task of finding more examples of the digraphs from the worksheet in their reading books.

Hook a word

Captain Hook went to look
For a word to rhyme with **rook**

Word shop

Shop for words with 'ar' in them.

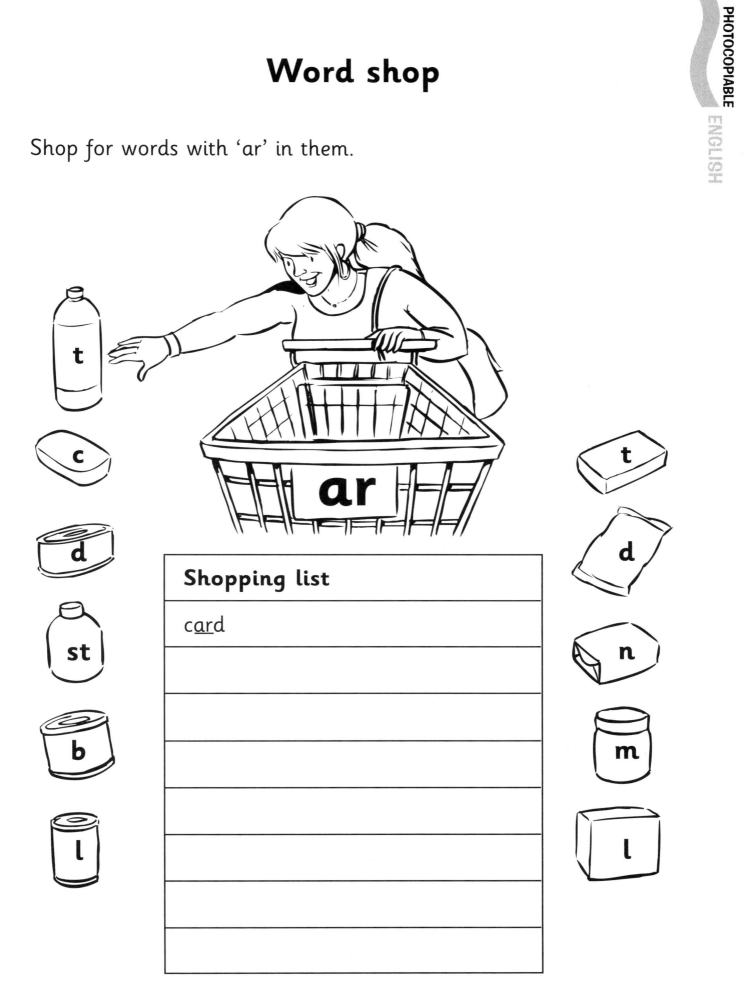

Shopping list

c<u>ar</u>d

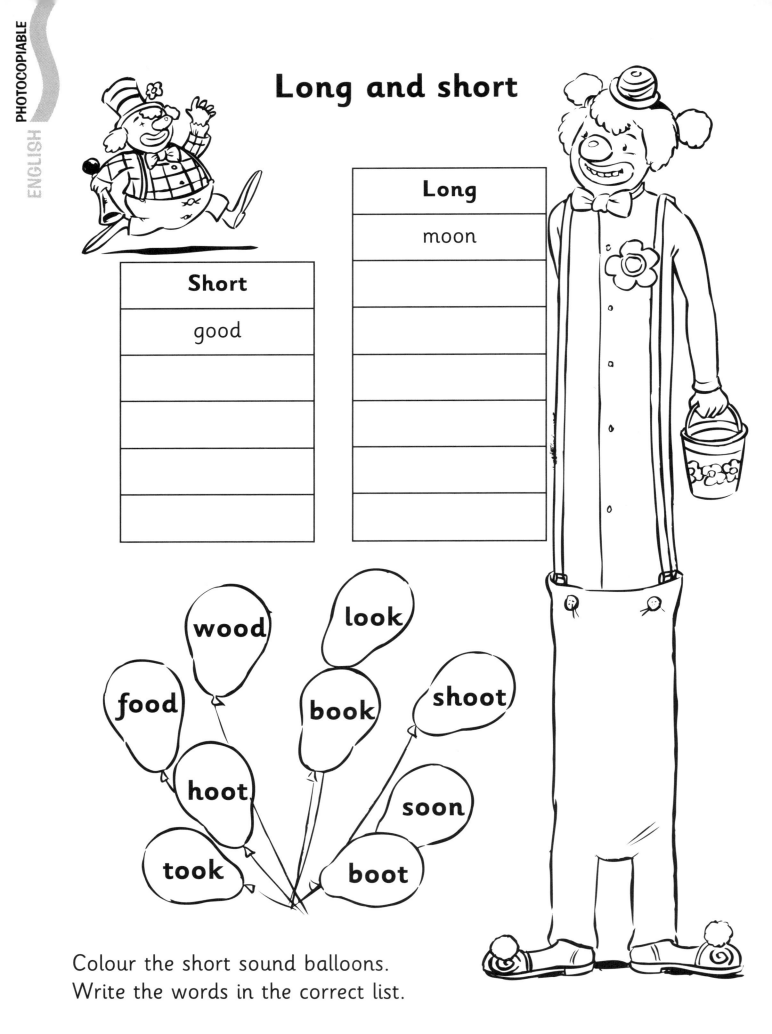

Long and short

Short
good

Long
moon

wood

look

food

book

shoot

hoot

soon

took

boot

Colour the short sound balloons.
Write the words in the correct list.

Top-up with oil

Add oil to make words.

s   t   b   d   f   c   r   sp

____oil

oil

Ship ahoy!

Make words with 'oy' in them.

-oy chart

Ow!

Complete the 'ow' words

Make and say

Can you make and say words with 'ou' in them?

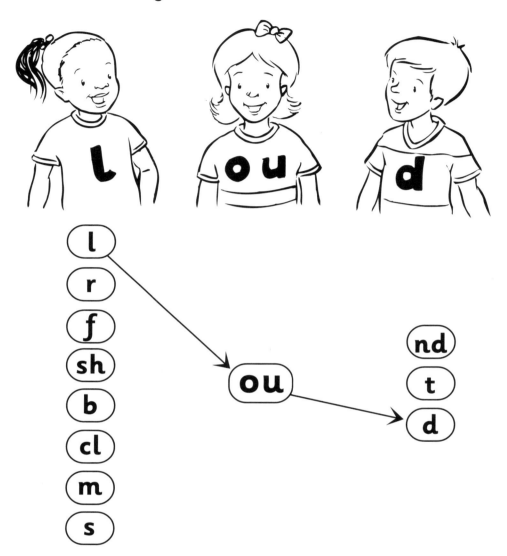

Write the words you make, and say them.

Picture links (1)

Link the picture in the frame to the other pictures that sound like **foot**.

Picture links (2)

Link the picture in the frame to the other pictures that sound like **dart**.

Picture links (3)

Link the picture in the frame to the other pictures that sound like **boy**.

Say and sort (1)

Say and sort (2)

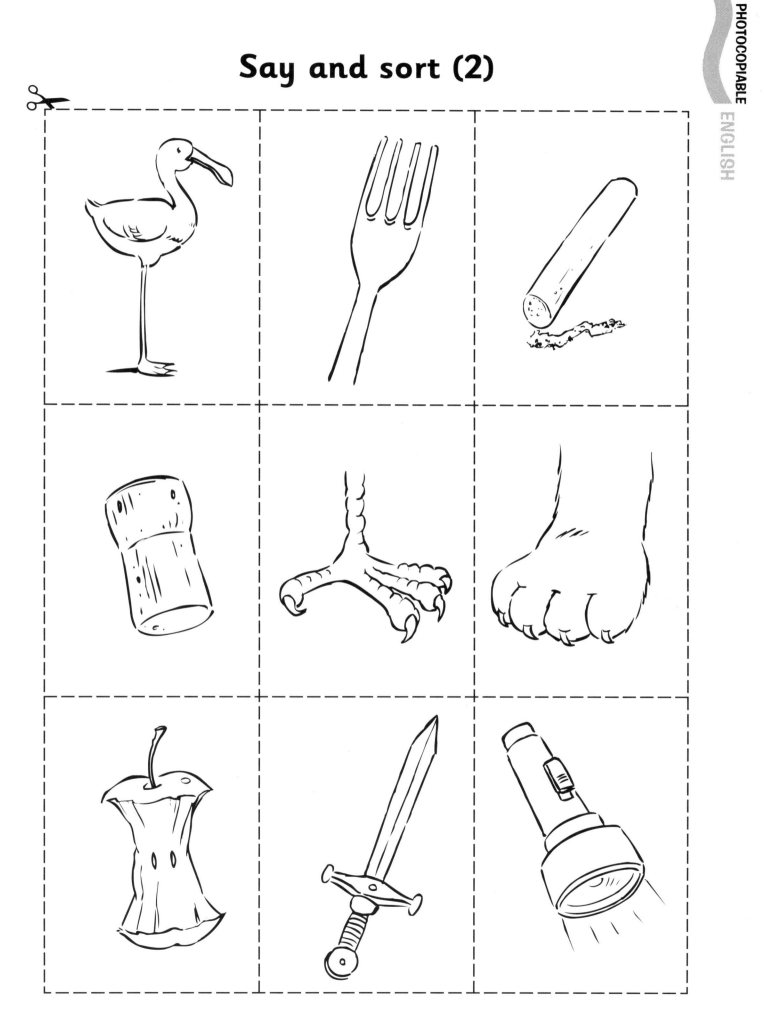

Say and sort (3)

Odd word out

Colour the odd word out in each group.

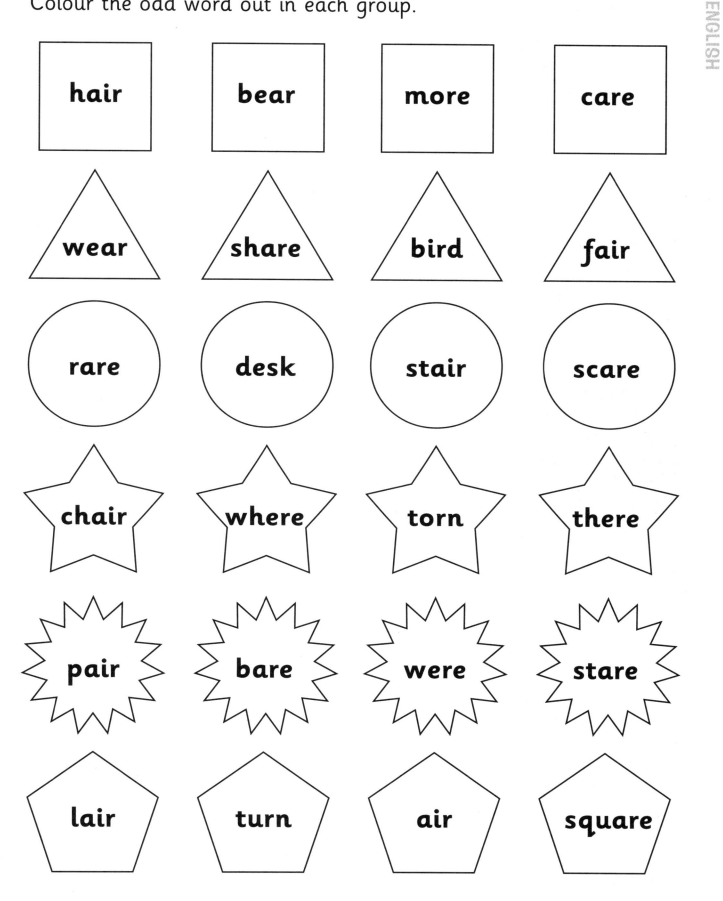

hair	bear	more	care
wear	share	bird	fair
rare	desk	stair	scare
chair	where	torn	there
pair	bare	were	stare
lair	turn	air	square

A necklace of rhymes

Colour words that rhyme with **fear** in blue.
Colour words that rhyme with **dead** in red.

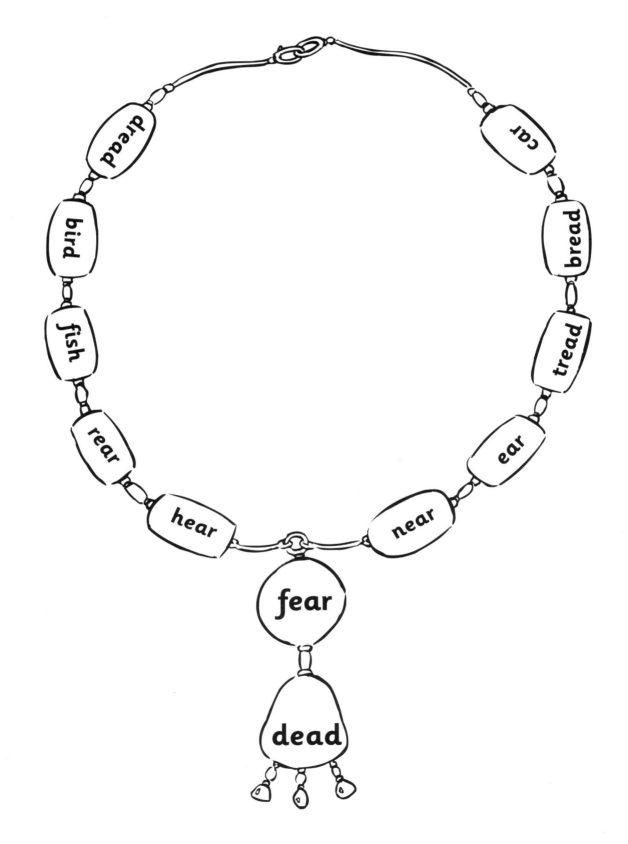

I went to town...

I went to town and...
_____

new shoes

rain

I went to town but...
_____

money

I went to town because...
_____

birthday

o'clock

I went to town until...
_____

park

I went to town although...
_____

shopping

Joined-up thinking

I ate my breakfast then...

I played football...

I watched television before...

I went to my friend's house after...

...I went to bed.

...fell fast asleep.

...morning playtime.

...school had ended.

...I walked to school.

Join these sentences and write them below.

Story starts

Finish these sentences.

Once upon a time

It started when

Suddenly

On Monday, Dan

Write a beginning of your own.

Dreamtime

Suddenly the ghost _____

_____

_____

When the dragon cried ____

_____

_____

After that I _____

_____

_____

Meanwhile, the car _____

_____

rode my bike
all the way
home.

made loud
banging
noises.

jumped out
of the TV.

he made a
big puddle.

What happened yesterday?

Choose the correct word to make each sentence.

Yesterday...

...Mum (went / goes) shopping.

_____

...Ali (falls / fell) off his scooter.

_____

...we all (go / went) to school.

_____

...Dad (jumps / jumped) into the pool.

_____

...I (started / start) to clean my bike.

_____

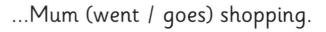

Mix and make families of words

good-

to-

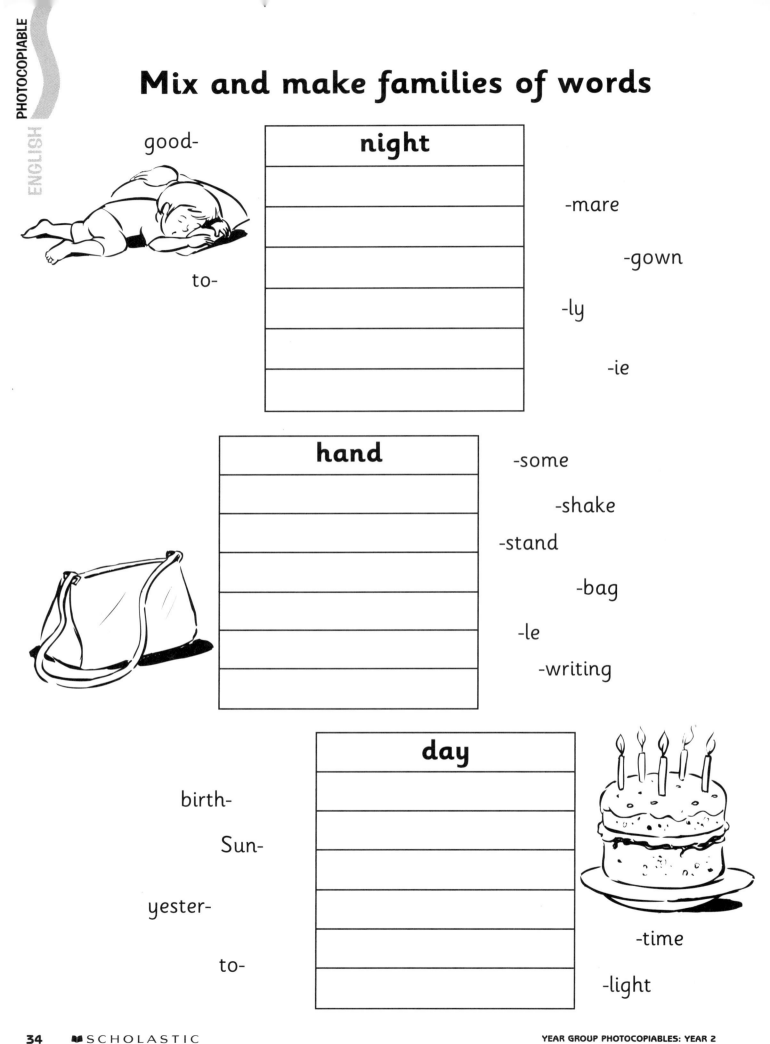

night

-mare

-gown

-ly

-ie

hand

-some

-shake

-stand

-bag

-le

-writing

birth-

Sun-

yester-

to-

day

-time

-light

Shopping lists

Commas are used to write lists.
Complete these shopping lists.

I went to market and bought _____,

_____, _____ and _____.

a hat   a pair of shoes   a bowl   a jug

We went to the garden centre and bought _____,

_____, _____ and _____.

a flowerpot   a trowel   a gnome   bulbs

She went to the seaside and bought _____

_____.

a postcard   a lolly   a bucket   a windmill

Write a sentence of your own on the back of the sheet.

Comma connections

Join these strips to make sentences. Write out the sentences, using a comma to join the parts.

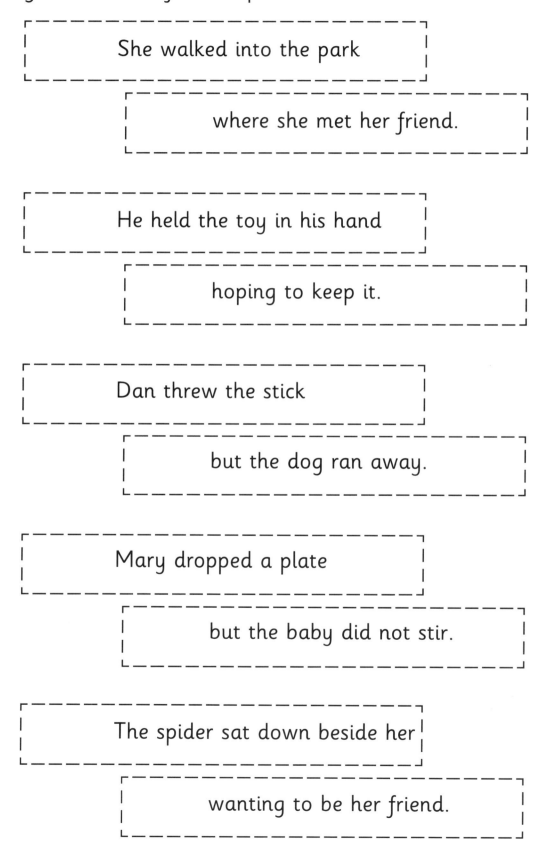

She walked into the park

where she met her friend.

He held the toy in his hand

hoping to keep it.

Dan threw the stick

but the dog ran away.

Mary dropped a plate

but the baby did not stir.

The spider sat down beside her

wanting to be her friend.

Asking questions: What? Where? When? Who?

Write a question to match each answer.

Answer	Question
Adam wore a red cap.	What did Adam wear?
Adam went to school.	Where _____?
Adam's birthday was on Monday.	When _____?
Auntie Jean kissed Adam.	Who _____?
Molly ate a green apple.	What _____?
Molly played at home.	Where _____?
Molly cried this morning.	When _____?
Molly loved her gran.	Who _____?

Sorting syllables (1)

Tap out the syllables, then sort the cards into sets.

dog

kan–ga–roo

kitt–en

snake

el–e–phant

ea–gle

mouse

cow

po–ny

rat

cro–co–dile

chick–en

ra–bbit

ca–mel

Sorting syllables (2)

Tap out the syllables, then sort the cards into sets.

spi–der

ko–a–la

tor–toise

oc–to–pus

squi–rrel

li–on

swan

gi–raffe

duck

fox

scor–pi–on

don–key

star–fish

but–ter–fly

At the party

This party is noisy! Add the question marks, and colour in the questions.

Making sense

Fill in the gaps with **new** words. Make sense!

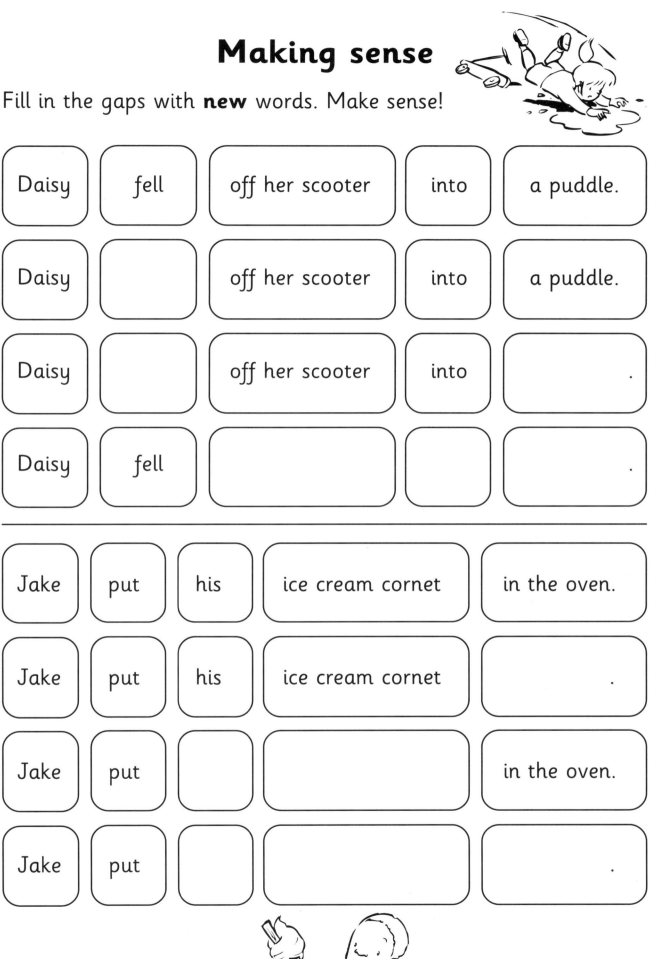

Daisy	fell	off her scooter	into	a puddle.
Daisy		off her scooter	into	a puddle.
Daisy		off her scooter	into	.
Daisy	fell			.

Jake	put	his	ice cream cornet	in the oven.
Jake	put	his	ice cream cornet	.
Jake	put			in the oven.
Jake	put			.

Yesterday, in the pond

Underline the correct words in the story.

Yesterday, I (see / saw) a

dog jump into the pond. A

boy threw (his / her) stick

into the pond for the dog to

(catch / caught). Three little

girls (was / were)

watching. They laughed.

One girl took (his / her)

shoes off and paddled in

the water. She (fell / fall) over and got very wet.

I (watch / watched) her mum wrap (him / her) in

a towel. She (was / were) very

cross. Then it started to rain,

so I (go / went) home.

Mandy's muddled messages

Can you un-muddle Mandy's messages?

to the zoo. My me took dad

_____

_____

_____

_____

_____

_____

ice creams. two I ate

sick. I was

_____

_____

_____

_____

_____

a lion? Have you seen ever

I best. the parrots liked

_____

_____

Angry Andy

Write about Andy

Wh – ch – ph

| wh**ite** | **ch**eap | alp**h**abet |

Say the words. Fill the gaps.

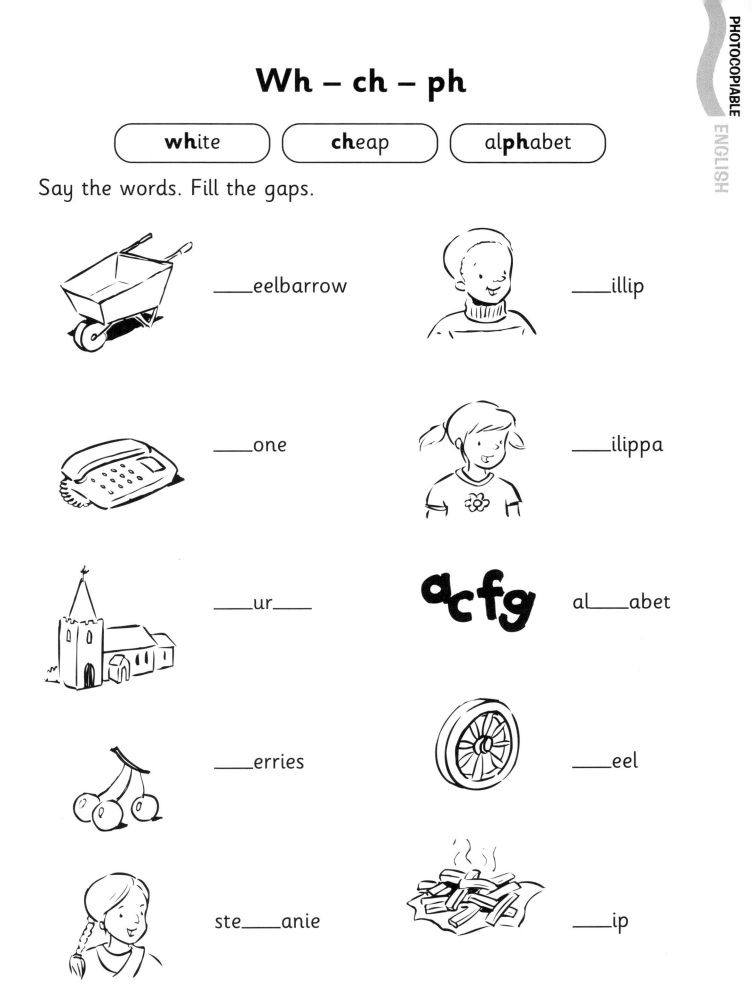

___eelbarrow

___illip

___one

___ilippa

___ur___

al___abet

___erries

___eel

ste___anie

___ip

MATHS

In Year 2 mathematics there is a great deal of emphasis placed on mental maths, rather than pencil and paper methods. Children are asked to master the rapid recall of number facts in multiplication and division, and they should also learn and practise mental calculation strategies.

In compiling this material we have tried to ensure that these processes are supported, although where pencil and paper are proscribed we feel it would be obtuse to adopt a worksheet approach. This has helped in selecting the material to be covered in this section, although quite a lot has had to be left out because the curriculum is so large. Mental calculation is generally avoided, although hopefully not the use of the brain. We have also largely ignored those areas where 'hands-on' is generally better than worksheet, for example when dealing with 3-D shapes, movement, and direction and data-collection.

The focus of the sheets is predominantly on number, the basic approach being to reinforce and confirm the fundamentals of number on which future learning can build. That is not to say that the worksheets only cover the 'easy stuff' – the mathematics prescribed for Year 2, and exemplified in the Numeracy Strategy documentation, is a progressive and demanding programme.

Group and tally (1) (page 53)

Objective: To count collections of objects by grouping in twos, fives or tens.

What to do: Talk to the children about ways of counting large numbers of objects. Show them how slow it can be to count one object at a time – can they think of a better way? Demonstrate the counting of objects in twos, fives and tens (perhaps by counting the children in the class).

Ask the children to count each set of pictures on the worksheet by grouping the objects as you demonstrated, in twos, fives or tens depending on the children's ability. They will need to keep a tally of their counting, making a mark for each group of objects that they count. (NB: Although 'tallying' is often used in a specific way to describe counting in bundles of five, it actually means making a mark to correspond to any given number so that one doesn't lose count.)

Differentiation: Provide counters or bricks for the less able so they can physically group objects for counting. Some children will find it sufficient to simply circle the groups on the sheet, then count the number of groups.

Extension: Challenge the children to count a set number of objects (say 33 stars on a sheet) in different ways, using groups of 10, 5 and 2. Ask: *Will you always*

get the same answer? Which method do you think will be quickest? Practise the 'group and count' strategy as often as possible in real situations in the classroom (the number of dinners, the number of paintbrushes and so on).

Group and tally (2) (page 54)

Objective: To count collections of objects by grouping in twos, fives or tens.

What to do: Look at the worksheet with the children, and ask them to group, tally and record their answers as they did with the previous sheet. This time, they will need to decide which grouping is the most appropriate for the task.

Differentiation: Once again the provision of counting apparatus, such as beads or counters, is the best support to provide for the less able.

Extension: Ask children to keep a suitable 'tally' (for example, of the number of cars passing the school, or the number of birds visiting the bird table) and to group and record the totals.

Keeping track (page 55)

Objective: To describe and extend number sequences by counting on and back on a number track.

What to do: Look together at the number lines on the worksheet. Ask the children to count the numbers they can see, then to continue extending the number line verbally, before locating the answers to the questions on each number line and writing them in position. Having gone forward, they should work backwards to complete the sequence of numbers.

Differentiation: Let less able children refer to a class number line. Don't make the referral too easy or this will become a copying exercise – if they have to leave their position to consult the line and then return to insert the numbers this should be sufficient. Encourage more able children to fill in all the numbers in the number line, and to continue counting beyond the numbers on the sheet.

Extension: Get the children to practise counting out loud, forwards and backwards from any number less than 101. This could be played as a game, with one child providing the starting number and direction for another to count. It would also make a good game to play at home.

Counting on or back (page 56)

Objective: To describe and extend number sequences on or back.

What to do: This is a simple 'question and answer' activity. The children will need to keep a tally of how many steps they have counted through when answering the questions.

Differentiation: Let less able children refer to a number line. The exercise can be reduced in difficulty by restricting the counting to smaller numbers only. Challenge more able children with harder questions.

Extension: Try the same questions as a mental exercise, played as a class game or homework game. Ask one child to count (say, back from 25 to 17), then ask the class: *How many did he count?*

Number vests (page 57)

Objective: To recognise one number as larger than another number.

What to do: Show the children how to select two digits from the runners' vests, writing them down in any order (this is best done on scrap paper to avoid confusion). The two remaining numbers on the vests should also be written down, in any order, on another piece of scrap paper. Ask the children to compare the two numbers, decide which is the larger number and record that in the first space on the sheet before completing the sentence with the second, smaller number. You might like to try re-using a digit in both numbers (thus you could have 54 is larger than 45). Ask the children to complete the sentences on the sheet with their own choice of numbers.

Differentiation: This activity is suitable for most Year 2 children, but you might like to provide the numbers on cards for less able children to manipulate and create two-digit numbers.

Extension: For homework, provide this puzzle: how many two-digit numbers can be made using the four digits? What difference does it make if you are allowed to use a digit twice in the same number?

Answers: Possible numbers are 45, 46, 47, 54, 56, 57, 64, 65, 67, 74, 75, 76. If duplicating digits is allowed, 44, 55, 66, and 77 are also allowed.

Jumping in tens (page 58)

Objective: To count on or back in tens from any number.

What to do: Look at the worksheet together. Ask: *What is the frog doing?* (Jumping in tens.) Explain to the children that they should continue jumping in tens for each of the questions on the sheet, writing the numbers into the boxes.

Differentiation: Being able to see the sequence of numbers is an asset, so give the less able a number square or number line. Blank number squares are particularly useful if children colour in the sequences so the pattern becomes clearer.

Extension: Oral practice is very worthwhile. Challenge members of the class to count on or back from a given number (out loud) in tens.

Odd and even numbers (page 59)

Objective: To recognise odd and even numbers.

What to do: Ask the children to colour in the even numbers on the number line (this is a reprise of work they should have covered earlier). They should then be able to complete the rest of the sheet as directed.

Differentiation: Children who have not grasped the 'evens' sequence may need to have the pattern pointed out to them. Try chanting in twos, or looking at a large number line – what do they notice about even numbers? More able children could recite odd and even numbers beyond those on the sheet.

Extension: Set children the task of collecting even numbers they meet in the real world: Which TV channels are even? Which classes are even numbers? Whose house is an even number? Which cars in the car park have even numbers on their number plates?

Number patterns (page 60)

Objective: To recognise and describe number sequences.

What to do: There is quite a lot of text on this worksheet, so it is as well to discuss numbers and number sequences beforehand, making sure that the children understand what they have to do. Suggest that they colour the squares lightly so the numbers are not completely obscured.

Differentiation: All children should manage this activity, but some may need help in describing the patterns that are produced. These children could work in a group, discussing their work with an adult.

Extension: Provide a selection of blank number squares (or perhaps pre-printed with numbers) and let children explore the different patterns they can make. Children could explore patterns made by fives, tens or threes.

Count and rule (page 61)

Objective: To describe and recognise familiar multiples.

What to do: Explain that the child on the left is reciting a number sequence, and the child on the right is explaining how the pattern is made. Look at the first example, then ask the children to do the same with the other examples.

Differentiation: Remove the need to write the explanation down, or simplify it for the less able. For example they could simply write 'add 3' or explain their reasoning orally to an adult.

Extension: Ask children to make up two sequences of their own for a friend to solve. The more able may well produce more demanding and interesting sequences, which you could discuss with the class.

Multiples in the air (page 62)

Objective: To begin to recognise familiar multiples.

What to do: This sheet assumes some understanding of the word 'multiple', which should have been introduced to the children before tackling a sheet like this to reinforce familiarity with it. The children should follow the instructions on the sheet. Read them through together if necessary.

Differentiation: Providing a visual prompt is probably the best form of differentiation for the less able – let them refer to a number line or square. If necessary, they could colour the sequence of multiples on the number line first. The more able will notice that there is more than one answer to some of the questions (40 is a multiple of 10, 5, 2 – and other numbers that the children may not yet have dealt with in multiples – 4 and 8).

Extension: Ask the children to draw a balloon race, where all the balloons are multiples of 3 (or another chosen number).

Words and numbers (page 63)

Objective: To read and write numbers in figures and words.

What to do: Explain the cartoon at the top: show that 'six' and '6' are different ways of reading and writing the same number. The children should then complete the number sentences on the rest of the sheet.

Differentiation: Give less able children access to a word bank of some sort. Some may find the action of writing the words difficult; for practice, the numbers could simply be copied as they are, and not translated from words to digits. Challenge very able children to read and write some numbers over 100.

Extension: Choose a decade and ask the children to write its numbers out in words (for example, for the 30s: thirty, thirty-one, thirty-two and so on).

Tens and units (page 64)

Objective: To know what each digit in a two-digit number represents and to be able to partition into tens and units.

What to do: Explain the sheet to the class. Draw attention to the fact that, in the top section of the sheet, they are trying to make only two-digit door numbers. Ask: *How many can you make? Could you make any other numbers?* For the rest of the sheet, the children should fill in the blanks as described.

Differentiation: Some children may find it helpful to use a 'try sheet' to try out numbers. In order to complete the last section children will need to have some understanding of place value. If they are struggling with this, let them tackle the questions using props – unit cubes, colour rods and so on – so they can physically divide the numbers into tens and units.

Extension: Carry out similar exercises orally. Ask: *What does the 5 represent in 57?* You cannot give the children too much practice at partitioning numbers.

Make a date (page 65)

Objective: To be able to recognise dates.

What to do: The children should write their own key dates at the top of the sheet. Underneath, ask the children to complete the three lists, one for each of the three months listed, identifying and recording the circled dates.

Differentiation: Some children will need support in working out what is required (in terms of -th -rd -st -nd endings). Provide help by getting them to say the dates out loud to an adult before writing them down on the sheet.

Extension: For homework, ask the children to record the birthdays of three friends or family (the year need not be included!)

More or less (page 66)

Objective: To compare two given numbers and to say which is more or less.

What to do: The children need to understand the vocabulary of comparison used before they can tackle this sheet. Work through the first example together, then ask the children to fill in the rest of the sheet as directed. Note that the last question has more than one possible answer (15, 16, 17, or 18), because it does not ask for the 'halfway' number.

Differentiation: Support the less able by providing apparatus – counters or cubes, for example – so that they can replicate the quantities and see the answers for themselves.

Extension: Plenty of oral work in the classroom is needed. Take every opportunity to use the words of comparison (refer to the Numeracy Strategy's

Mathematical Vocabulary booklet for lists) in the classroom. Set problems, based around the classroom, for the children to solve: *Which class has the most children – class X or class Y?*

Ten more or ten less (page 67)

Objective: To say what number is ten more or less than a given number.

What to do: Make sure the children understand the instructions on the sheet, reading them through together if necessary. Ask the children to work out the answers and to then complete the questions on the sheet.

Differentiation: Provide number squares or number lines to those that need them. In order to complete the fragment of the number square, you could supply a printed hundred square and ask children to draw around the section identified on the sheet.

Extension: Challenge children to complete other fragments of a hundred square that you supply. This could be a homework task.

Estimate and count (page 68)

Objective: To begin to use and understand the vocabulary of estimation.

What to do: You will need to do some work before this activity, introducing the children to some strategies for estimation – remind them that it is not just guesswork! Get them to 'chunk' objects into rough sets of 5 or 10 to practise estimation: *How many children in the playground? How many windows in the school? How many tiles on the classroom floor?* Make sure that the instructions 'estimate', 'count' and 'difference' are understood before they complete the sheet.

Differentiation: You may need to provide help in counting accurately. Remind the children of ways of tallying – it is easy to lose count of scattered spots!

Extension: As homework, ask the children to estimate, count and find the difference between the two for problems such as: *The number of houses in my street; The number of cars in the car park; The number of tiles on the bathroom wall* and so on.

Rounding to ten (page 69)

Objective: To round a number to the nearest ten.

What to do: Explain the term 'rounding' to the children, using the first question on the sheet as an example. Point out how they can see that 23 is closer to 20 than 30 on the number line. Ask the children to complete the sheet as instructed.

Differentiation: Less able children could work with a large number line, finding the position on the line then

seeing which 'ten' number is closer to it.

Extension: Provide numbers for children to round to the nearest ten, without the aid of a number line.

Halves and quarters (1) (page 70)

Objective: To recognise and write ½, ¼, and one half and one quarter.

What to do: The sheet is self-explanatory, although it might be worthwhile drawing some shapes on the board and dividing them into halves and quarters with the children first, so they are familiar with what they should be looking for in the shapes on the worksheet.

Differentiation: Some children may find this a very difficult exercise, especially if they have had little experience of fractions. Support these children through demonstration (cutting apples, sharing a cake and so on). An adult could work with less confident children on the sheet, perhaps enlarging the sheet and cutting out the fractions so that the child can see how each fraction is the same by matching pieces of the shape.

Extension: Provide more experience of dealing with halves and quarters. Use plastic and wooden shapes and games (these can be purchased from educational suppliers, or made from stiff card) to provide hands-on experience of fractions.

Halves and quarters (2) (page 71)

Objective: To find a half or a quarter of even numbers below 20.

What to do: Recap on work on fractions, looking at the work carried out in the previous activity. Look together at the worksheet, and ask the children to divide each group on the sheet into the fractions indicated. You might like to ask the children to colour each proportion of the objects in a different colour.

Differentiation: Help less able children to divide groups up by using real objects (counters or cubes are a good example).

Extension: Pose children the problem of finding a half or a quarter of just a number, rather than a group of objects. Give whole even numbers only, asking: *What is half of 18?* and so on.

Fractions (1) (page 72)

Objective: To recognise and find ½ of even numbers below 20, and to recognise what is not a half.

What to do: This activity will develop the children's awareness of fractions. Explain the sheet, and ask the children to circle the pictures that are clearly not halves, which is straightforward. However, they need to provide an explanation as to how they know what is a half and what isn't. A verbal answer to this question is best, so ask the children to talk to an adult about their work when they reach this point. The rest of the sheet requires the blanks to be completed.

Differentiation: Let the less able work with real objects in order to find halves. The first part can easily be replicated with objects. Provide adult support for children to talk the problems through with, and to help in the explanation of what they think a half is.

Extension: Take every opportunity to provide more practice of similar problems, and experience of fractions in real-life situations. Ask children to report any sightings or uses of fractions that they encounter over, say, a weekend. ('My mum bought half a dozen eggs; Dad said he had half a tank of petrol; The chocolate was divided into four equal quarters.')

Fractions (2) (page 73)

Objective: To recognise the equivalence between simple fractions.

What to do: This worksheet builds on the previous activity, introducing the identification of quarters as well as halves. Make sure that children understand the instructions on the sheet as reading may be a problem. Read through the questions together if necessary.

Differentiation: Provide apparatus (such as sets of shapes divided into fractions, which are commercially available) for children to manipulate and to help them

appreciate, by handling, the equivalence of the fractions described on the worksheet.

Extension: Pose more simple fraction problems based upon halves and quarters for children to discuss: *What do three quarters and one quarter make? What do two halves make? What does one half and one quarter make?* Provide simple apparatus to support children that need it.

Halfway (page 74)

Objective: To begin to position halves along a number line.

What to do: This activity will help the children relate work on halves and quarters to their place value in the number system. Use the first completed example on

the worksheet to explain the task. Talk with the children about adding a half to a number – this could be done with a group or the whole class, perhaps using a number line on the board to show where the number would be positioned. Children can then complete the sentences on the sheet in the same fashion.

Differentiation: A ruler, ideally with halves marked, can be used to provide support for the less able. Show them how to recreate the questions on the ruler, where the halfway division will be clearer.

Extension: Provide further problems to solve without the aid of a number line or ruler, for example: *What is halfway between 45 and 46? 27 and 28? 99 and 100?*

Three hops (page 75)

Objective: To use a number line to add three numbers.

What to do: Go through the first example carefully with the children. It is not as easy as it looks, because it involves careful counting of the jumps as well as recording in a number sentence. Explain that the square and the triangle stand for (different) unknown numbers in each of the questions on the sheet.

In making their own jumps they can, of course, use equal steps: 6 + 7 + 7 = 20 (which might be posed as 6+ ☐ + ☐ = 20). Let children use the number line freely to sketch in the jumps, encouraging them to use different colours for each of the three hops so that they can see their answers. If necessary, duplicate the sheet to provide further number lines for the children to use.

Differentiation: Groups of less able children could be supported by working together with an adult, perhaps using a large number line on a board to demonstrate the jumps. Some may find the exercise too fiddly on an A4 page, and may benefit from an enlarged copy of the worksheet.

Extension: Challenge children to find three hops to make 100. Alternatively, provide some examples with the middle hop missing (30 + ☐ + 60 = 100): *Can you find the missing jump?*

Less than (page 76)

Objective: To understand 'less than', and vocabulary related to subtraction.

What to do: Explain the sheet, paying particular attention to the need for the children to accurately count the number of objects given for comparison. Show them how to find the solution by subdividing the set of objects (taking away) and counting the remainder to provide the answer.

Differentiation: Once again, those children who find the activity difficult will need hands-on experience. Provide apparatus with which they can replicate the problems and physically carry out the operation of 'taking away', and allowing them to count what's left.

Extension: Provide real-life subtraction problems (money, measurement, objects) and discuss how the children might find the answers. This will help develop an understanding of subtraction as taking away, finding the difference between, and complementary addition. For example: *What is the difference between 15p and 7p? Take 7p from 15p. If I add 8p to a sum of money I have 15p, what was that sum of money?*

Lots of blanks (page 77)

Objective: To understand vocabulary related to the operation of multiplication.

What to do: Using the first completed example, demonstrate what is required on the sheet, then ask the children to fill in the rest of the blanks. Note that '3 lots of 2' is written as '3 × 2' in order to match the grammar of the written sentence. It can, of course, be written as '2 × 3', which is sometimes preferred mathematically but does not follow the sentence '3 lots of 2' in this example. (For exemplification see *The National Numeracy Strategy: More Numeracy Lessons*, DfEE, p46)

Differentiation: A peg board and pegs or cubes can be used for less able children to replicate the arrays drawn on the sheet.

Extension: Give children a peg board and ask them to create their own arrays, recording each in two different ways (for example, 5 × 6 = 30 and 6 × 5 = 30).

Sharing equally (page 78)

Objective: To understand the operation of division as sharing equally.

What to do: The children need to share each group of objects on the worksheet equally between the people (or animals) that have been drawn. The questions are presented in such a way that the children can share out the objects by drawing lines or groupings if they wish. They should also record the number of objects in each group at the side of the statements.

Differentiation: Show less able children how they can share objects by turning the activity into a practical one, giving the children objects (coins, apples and so on), and letting them share between a group of children who can pretend to be the characters on the worksheet.

Extension: Devise a problem for children to solve (perhaps at home). For example: *I have 16 oranges. How many bags of 2 oranges can I fill?* Lots of mental practice of division is needed: *Share 15 between three. How many tens make 30. Divide 8 by 4 and so on.*

Halves and doubles (page 79)

Objective: To begin to use and understand halves and doubles.

What to do: The children need to have been introduced to the concept of doubling and halving before this activity. Explain how the trails on the sheet work, and read the first example to the children (1, 2, 4, 8, 16, 32) to make sure they understand what they have to do to complete the sheet.

Differentiation: Help less able children by providing a number square, number line, board and pegs, or apparatus to aid counting such as cubes or buttons.

Extension: Ask the children to learn by heart the doubles of all numbers from 1 to 15.

The right sign (page 80)

Objective: To recognise and use correctly the +, −, × and ÷ signs.

What to do: It is worth explaining the cartoon at the top: signs must be correct! Ask the children: *What signs would make sense of these number sentences?* Try putting different symbols in the first few sums until the children get the idea of the exercise. The answers should be written in the spaces provided.

Differentiation: Once again, the less able would find hands-on experience of great benefit. Let them manipulate objects to try out their 'guesses', and ask questions as they go: *Does 7 + 4 = 3?*

Extension: Challenge the children to make puzzles of their own for a friend to try. They should construct the equation first, then blank out the operation sign.

Magic squares (page 81)

Objective: To reason using numbers.

What to do: This activity is best tackled initially by a group. Work through the first square on a board together, showing how each row, column and diagonal can be made to add up to the same total. Then let the children work individually on the second square. (The solution follows exactly the same pattern as the example.)

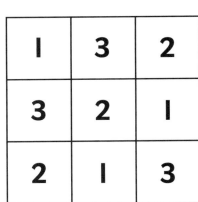

Differentiation: Having explained the first example to less able children, give them the same numbers (1, 2, 3) and a blank grid to see if they can replicate the example. When they then tackle the second puzzle they should be more able to see the pattern. If not, discuss the pattern with the child: *What do you notice about the diagonals in the first example?*

Extension: Can the children solve the same puzzle using the numbers 7, 8, and 9?

Problems (page 82)

Objective: To solve real life problems.

What to do: Make sure that the children can read and understand the questions. Let them do any working out that they need to on the paper.

Differentiation: Encourage less able children to record the quantities given in the questions, generating a number sentence, as this often makes the problem seem easier. Let them use counters to represent the apples and people so they can carry out the problem as a practical exercise.

Extension: Do simple puzzles as an oral exercise regularly; many problems of a similar nature should be tackled.

Measures (page 83)

Objective: To understand and begin to read and use the vocabulary of measures.

What to do: This sheet requires some advance knowledge of measures, as the children should be familiar with the units described. There should be visual displays in the classroom as an aid to the children's memories. Complete the first question together – a coloured line is used to connect the measure required to the appropriate unit of measurement – then ask the children to complete the sheet.

Differentiation: Provide adult support, and talk with children about what might be ridiculous answers: *Can I boil an egg for 3 metres?* Have the units of measurement on display so that the child can see them.

Extension: Play oral games with the class, throwing out regular challenges of a similar sort: *I have to fill my car with petrol. Shall I buy metres of petrol? I went to the supermarket and bought 5 hours of milk.* Can the children say what is wrong? What units should be used for each statement?

Centimetre lines (page 84)

Objective: To use a ruler to measure and draw lines that are a multiple of 1cm.

What to do: This activity must be properly demonstrated to the children before they work on this sheet, as children do not automatically know how to hold and use a ruler. You

will, of course, need good, clear, undamaged rulers for the children to use.

Differentiation: Some children will find the physical manipulation of a ruler very difficult. They will need an adult to help them by holding the equipment correctly, so that the child can still read the measurements from the ruler.

Extension: Challenge the children to measure the length of a number of everyday objects – a book, a shoe, a mouse mat, a telephone handset and so on. This could be done for homework.

Answers: 10cm, 7cm, 12cm, 3cm, 17cm.

On time (page 85)

Objective: To read the time to the half- or quarter-hour on a digital or analogue clock.

What to do: Ask the children to complete the sheet, using the first example to illustrate what they should do.

Differentiation: The best support for the less able is to provide teaching clocks (both analogue and digital) that they can manipulate and use to replicate the problems on the sheet.

Extension: Children will need lots of practice at reading the time, so provide more examples. Use an analogue clock, or a clock stamp, to pose questions for the class.

Lines of symmetry (page 86)

Objective: To recognise and draw a line of symmetry on simple shapes and outlines, and to complete a symmetrical pattern by drawing the other half.

What to do: Test the children's knowledge of what a line of symmetry is before carrying out this activity, and perhaps demonstrate an example on the board. For the first section of the sheet, those who can use a ruler can use one to draw the line of symmetry on the shape, but it is acceptable for the line to be drawn freehand. Complete the sheet as described.

Differentiation: Provide mirrors so that the children can test the lines of symmetry (safe, non-breakable mirrors are available for this purpose). They can then see when they are correct.

Extension: Give children peg boards on which to create their own symmetrical patterns, as in the examples at the bottom of the sheet. Set up the line of symmetry first, or ask the children to show where it is when they have completed their pattern.

Group and tally (1)

Count these sheep in twos.
Make a mark for every two you count.

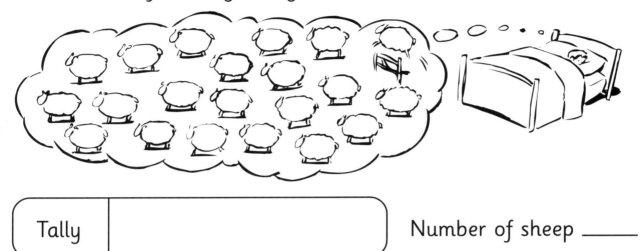

Tally	

Number of sheep _____

Count the bees in fives. Keep a tally as you count.

Tally	

Number of bees _____

Count these soldiers in tens. Keep a tally as you count.

Tally	

Number of soldiers _____

Group and tally (2)

Group these objects in twos, fives or tens. Keep a tally as you count the groups. For example:

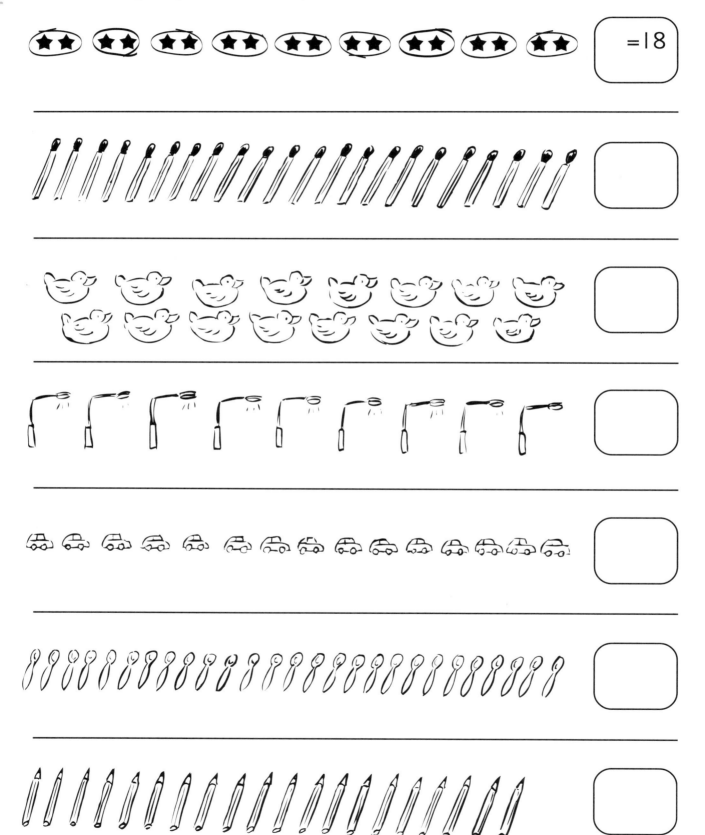

Keeping track

Where would 32 be? Write it on the line. Where would 24 be?

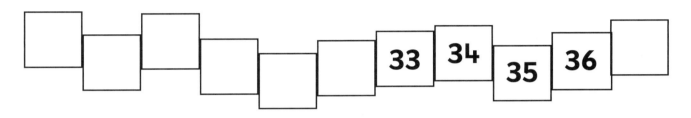

Where would 28, 31 and 37 be? Write them on the line.

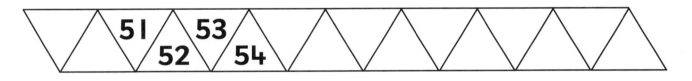

Where would 61, 57 and 49 be? Write them on the line.

Where would 82 be? What about 73 and 80?
Write them on the line.

Where would 100 be? What about 92, 90 and 99?
Write them on the line.

Counting on or back

Count on from 22 to 27.
How many did you count?

Count on from 31 to 36.
How many did you count?

Count back from 55 to 50.
How many did you count?

Count back from 68 to 62.
How many did you count?

Count on from 81 to 87.
How many did you count?

Count back from 78 to 72.
How many did you count?

Count on from 93 to 100.
How many did you count?

Count back from 11 to 0.
How many did you count?

Number vests

Make up numbers from the runners' vests on two cards. Say which is the larger number.

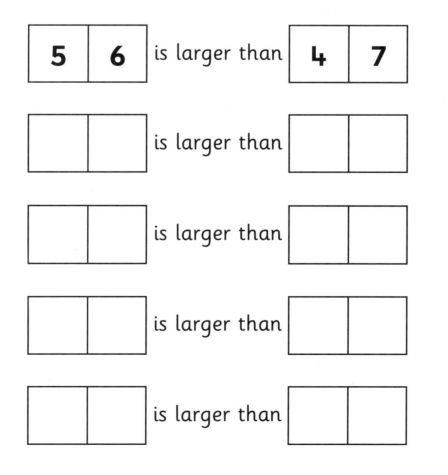

| 5 | 6 | is larger than | 4 | 7 |

is larger than

is larger than

is larger than

is larger than

Jumping in tens

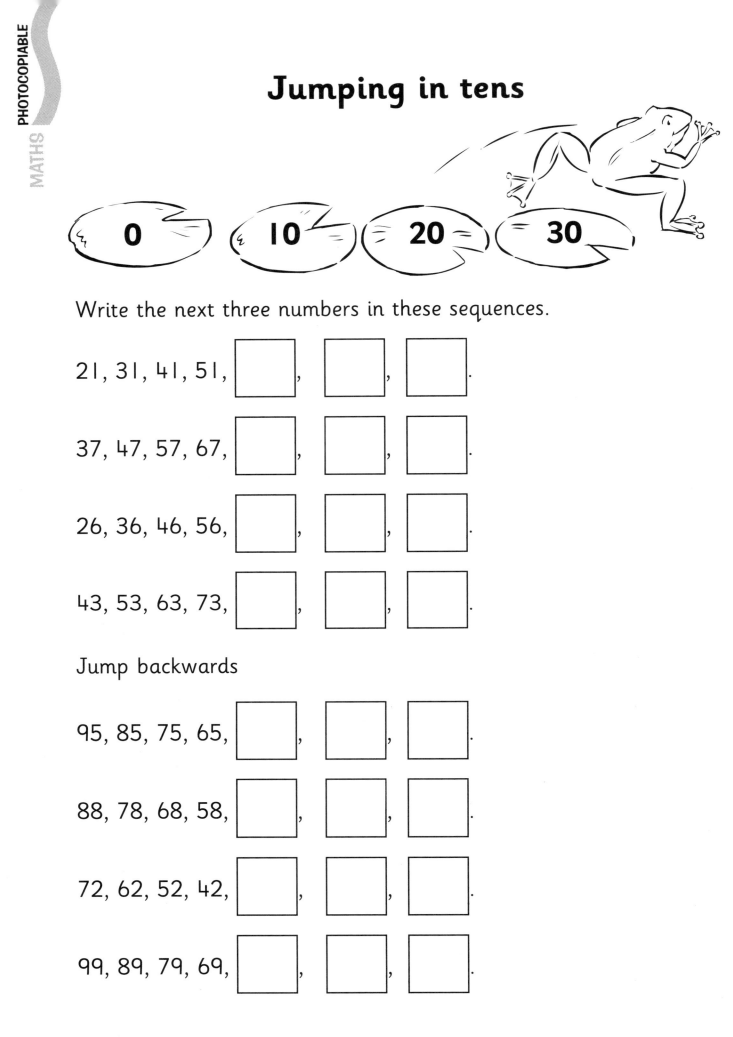

Write the next three numbers in these sequences.

21, 31, 41, 51, ☐ , ☐ , ☐ .

37, 47, 57, 67, ☐ , ☐ , ☐ .

26, 36, 46, 56, ☐ , ☐ , ☐ .

43, 53, 63, 73, ☐ , ☐ , ☐ .

Jump backwards

95, 85, 75, 65, ☐ , ☐ , ☐ .

88, 78, 68, 58, ☐ , ☐ , ☐ .

72, 62, 52, 42, ☐ , ☐ , ☐ .

99, 89, 79, 69, ☐ , ☐ , ☐ .

Odd and even numbers

1 2 3 4 5 6 7 8 9 10 11 12 13 14 15

Put a ring around every other number. What do you notice?

16 17 18 19 20 21 22 23 24 25 26 27 28 29 30

Colour in the balloons that have even numbers on them.

Continue the number sequences.

21, 23, 25, 27, ⬜ , ⬜ , ⬜ , ⬜ .

18, 20, 22, 24, ⬜ , ⬜ , ⬜ , ⬜ .

What odd number comes after 5? ⬜ .

Number patterns

1	2	3	4	5
6	7	8	9	10
11	12	13	14	15
16	17	18	19	20
21	22	23	24	25

Count on in twos. Start from 1. Colour each number you land on.

What sort of pattern have you made?

_____

What sort of pattern will you get on this bigger square?
Count on in twos and see.

1	2	3	4	5	6
7	8	9	10	11	12
13	14	15	16	17	18
19	20	21	22	23	24
25	26	27	28	29	30
31	32	33	34	35	36

Try making your own number square that's four squares wide.
What sort of pattern do you get this time?

Count and rule

Count   **Rule**

2, 4, 6, 8, 10...

Add 2 to each number to make the next one.

Complete the count and write down each rule.

3, 6, 9, 12, ☐, ☐ ...

10, 8, 6, ☐, ☐ ...

10, 15, 20, ☐, ☐ ...

Fill in the missing numbers.

17, 15, ☐, 11, 9 . . .

5, 10, 15, ☐, 25 . . .

3, ☐, 9, 12, 15 . . .

Multiples in the air

Colour the multiples of 10 in red.
Colour the multiples of 3 in green.
What do you notice about the other numbers?

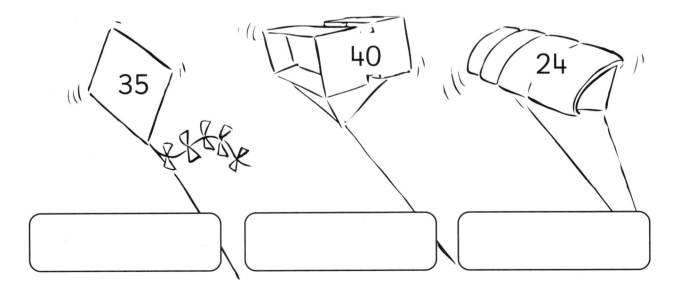

What numbers are these multiples of?

Words and numbers

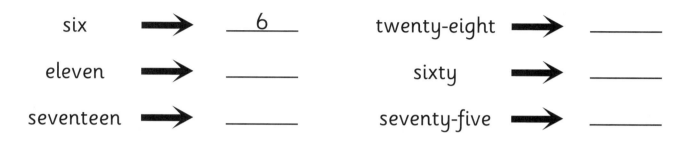

Write these words as numbers.

six   ➡   <u>6</u>   twenty-eight   ➡   _____

eleven   ➡   _____   sixty   ➡   _____

seventeen   ➡   _____   seventy-five   ➡   _____

Write these numbers in words.

39   ➡   <u>thirty-nine</u> _____

99   ➡   _____

32   ➡   _____

500   ➡   _____

12   ➡   _____

5   ➡   _____

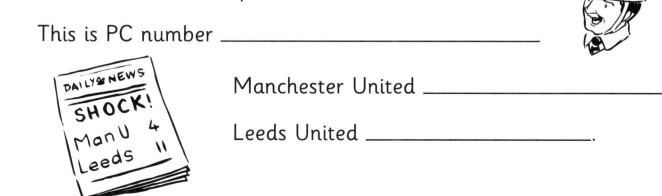

Write **words** to complete these sentences.

This is PC number _____

Manchester United _____,

Leeds United _____.

Tens and units

How many door numbers can you make using these three numbers? Use two numbers each time.

Say the numbers. Fill in the blanks.

21 = 20 + 1

35 = 30 + ☐

57 = 50 + ☐

42 = 40 + ☐

66 = 60 + ☐

83 = 80 + ☐

30 + 6 = ☐

90 + 2 = ☐

70 + 3 = ☐

20 + 1 = ☐

40 + 8 = ☐

50 + 7 = ☐

Split these numbers into tens and units.

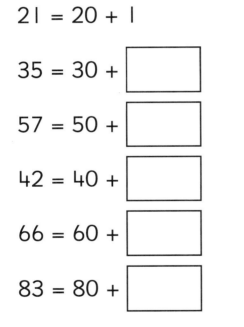

25 = ☐ + △

32 = ☐ + △

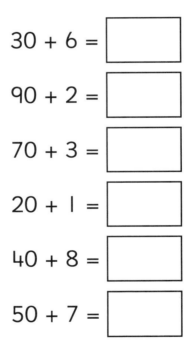

46 = ☐ + △

45 = ☐ + △

Make a date

My birthday is 29th October.

What date is your birthday? _____

What is today's date? _____

Write the dates circled on the calendar. The first one has been done for you.

3rd October _____   _____   _____

_____   _____   _____

_____   _____   _____

_____   _____   _____

_____   _____   _____

_____   _____   _____

■SCHOLASTIC   **65**

More or less

Sunita's book has 32 pages.

Manjot's book has 64 pages.

Whose book has the most pages? _____

Which is more, 58p or 85p? _____

Which is more, 41kg or 74kg? _____

Which is more, 25 or 52? _____

Jo's cake

Matt's cake

Whose cake has fewer candles? _____

What number lies halfway between 15 and 25? _____

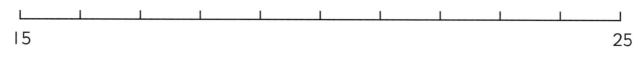

15   25

A number lies between 14 and 19. What could it be?

_____

Ten more or ten less

What number is 10 before 67? _____

What number is 10 after 67? _____

What number is 10 less than 81? _____

What number is 10 more than 23? _____

Fill in the missing numbers on this part of a hundred square.

4	5	6	7
	15		17
		26	

Write the missing numbers in the spaces.

	ten more is			**ten more is**	
31	➡	☐	☐	➡	20
44	➡	☐	☐	➡	25
53	➡	☐	☐	➡	41
62	➡	☐	☐	➡	55
87	➡	☐	☐	➡	99

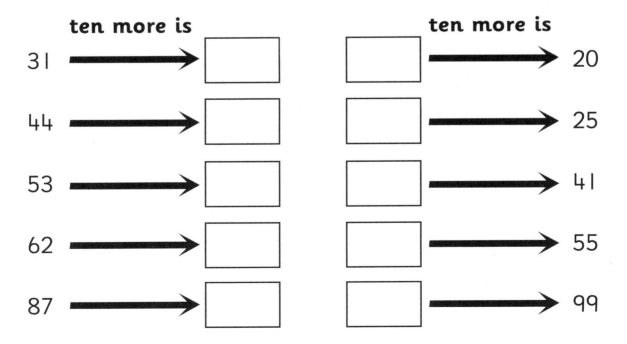

Estimate and count

Estimate each number, then count and record the actual number. What is the difference between the two numbers?

How many spots?

Estimate _____

Actual number _____

Difference _____

How many bricks?

Estimate _____

Actual number _____

Difference _____

How many books?

Estimate _____

Actual number _____

Difference _____

How many birds?

Estimate _____

Actual number _____

Difference _____

Rounding to ten

What is the nearest 10 to 23?

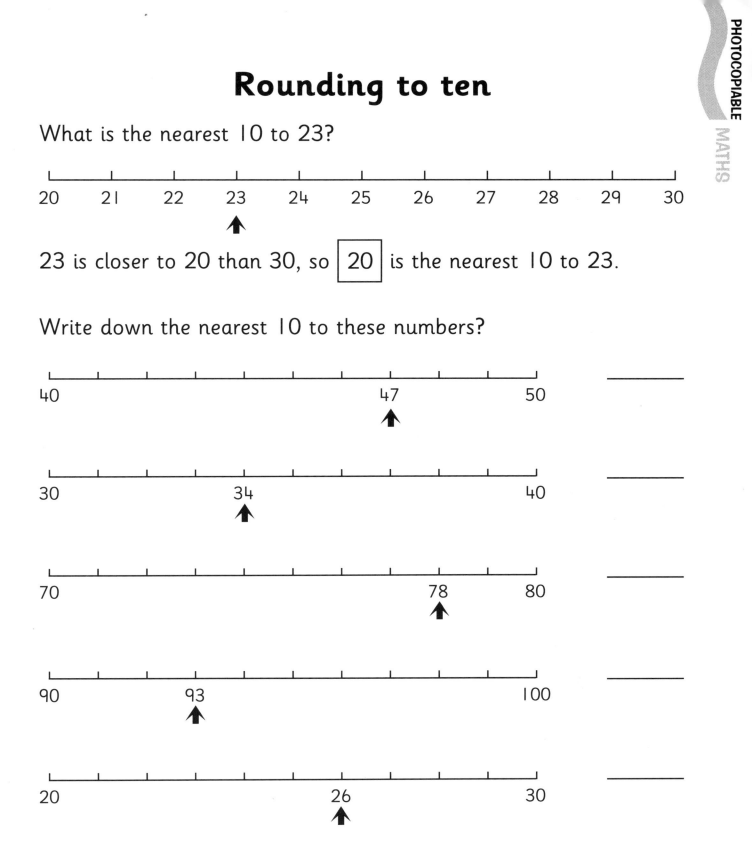

20	21	22	23	24	25	26	27	28	29	30

23 is closer to 20 than 30, so ⬛ 20 ⬛ is the nearest 10 to 23.

Write down the nearest 10 to these numbers?

| 40 | | | | | | 47 | | | 50 | _____ |

| 30 | | | 34 | | | | | | 40 | _____ |

| 70 | | | | | | 78 | | | 80 | _____ |

| 90 | | | 93 | | | | | | 100 | _____ |

| 20 | | | | | | 26 | | | 30 | _____ |

When the number is halfway between two tens, round up to the next ten.

| 10 | | | | 15 | | | | | 20 | _____ |

Halves and quarters (1)

Read and copy these sentences.

One whole = **1** _____

One half   = $\frac{1}{2}$ _____

One quarter = $\frac{1}{4}$ _____

What fraction of these shapes is shaded?

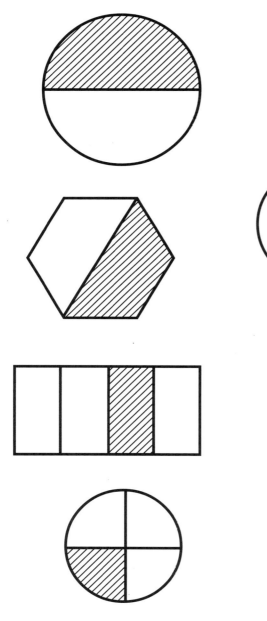

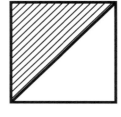

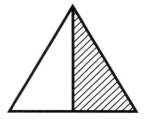

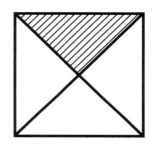

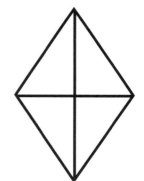

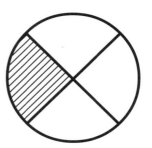

Halves and quarters (2)

Draw a line to divide these sets of objects **in half**.

Put a coloured line around **a quarter** of these objects.

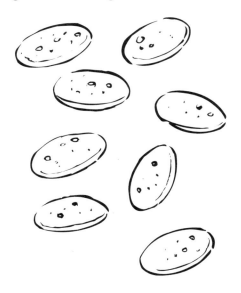

Fractions (1)

Draw a circle around the pictures that do not show a half.

How can you tell?

Answer these questions.

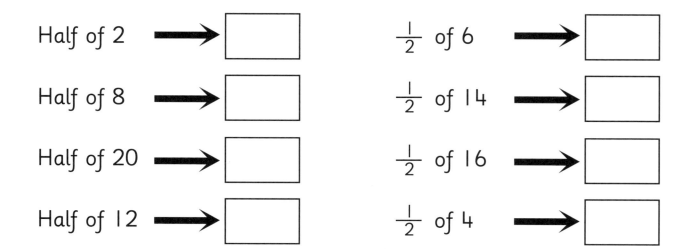

Half of 2 ➡️ ☐ $\frac{1}{2}$ of 6 ➡️ ☐

Half of 8 ➡️ ☐ $\frac{1}{2}$ of 14 ➡️ ☐

Half of 20 ➡️ ☐ $\frac{1}{2}$ of 16 ➡️ ☐

Half of 12 ➡️ ☐ $\frac{1}{2}$ of 4 ➡️ ☐

Fractions (2)

Copy these fractions

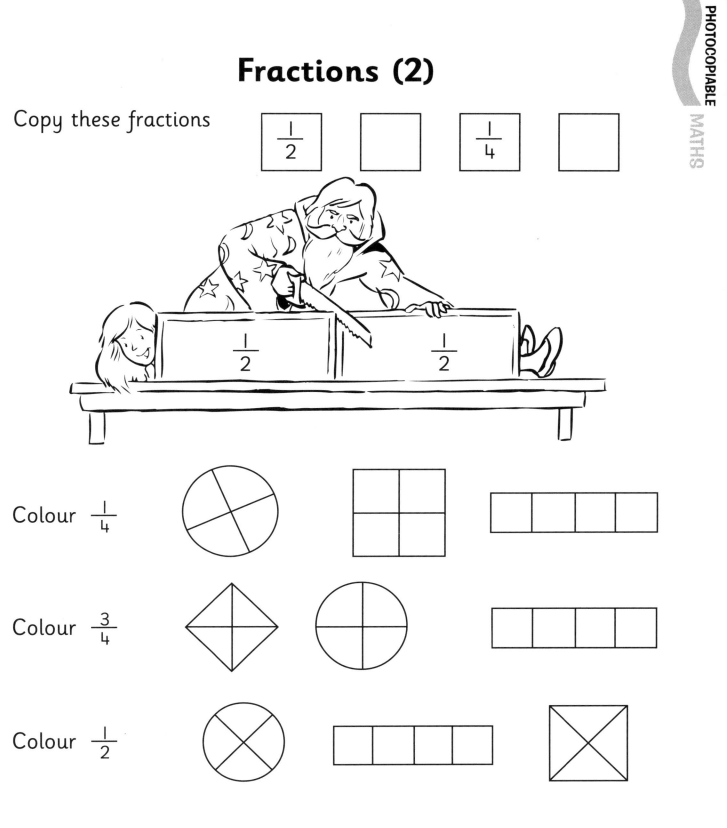

Colour $\frac{1}{4}$

Colour $\frac{3}{4}$

Colour $\frac{1}{2}$

How many quarters are the same as one half? _____

How many halves are the same as one whole? _____

How many quarters are the same as one whole? _____

Halfway

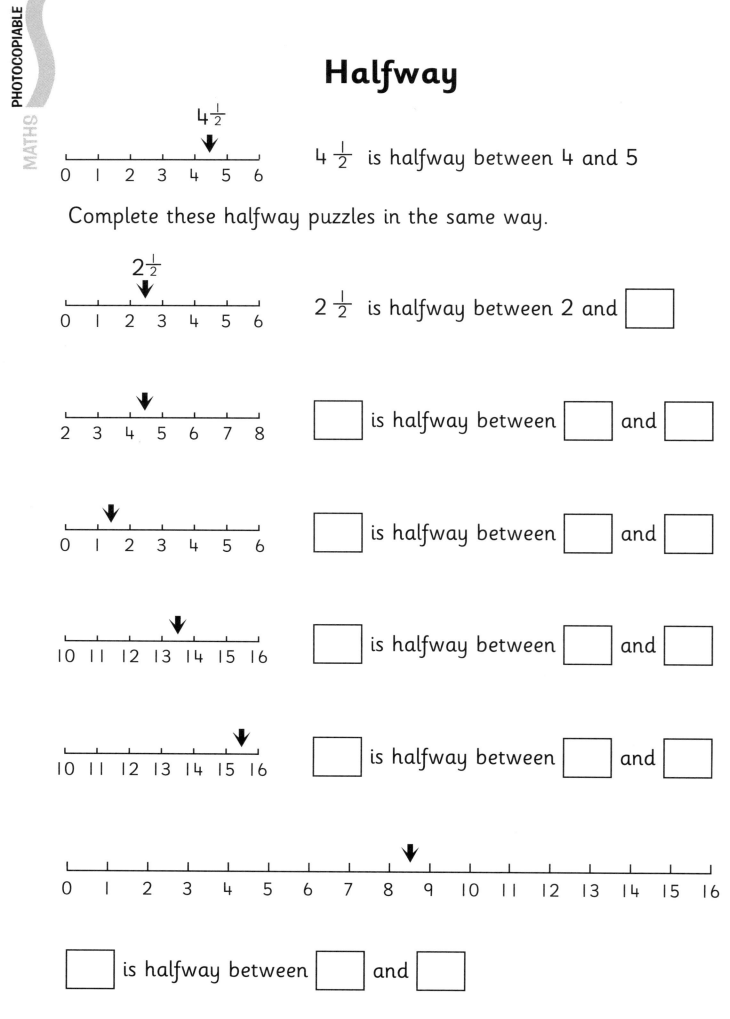

$4\frac{1}{2}$ is halfway between 4 and 5

Complete these halfway puzzles in the same way.

$2\frac{1}{2}$ is halfway between 2 and ☐

☐ is halfway between ☐ and ☐

☐ is halfway between ☐ and ☐

☐ is halfway between ☐ and ☐

☐ is halfway between ☐ and ☐

☐ is halfway between ☐ and ☐

Three hops

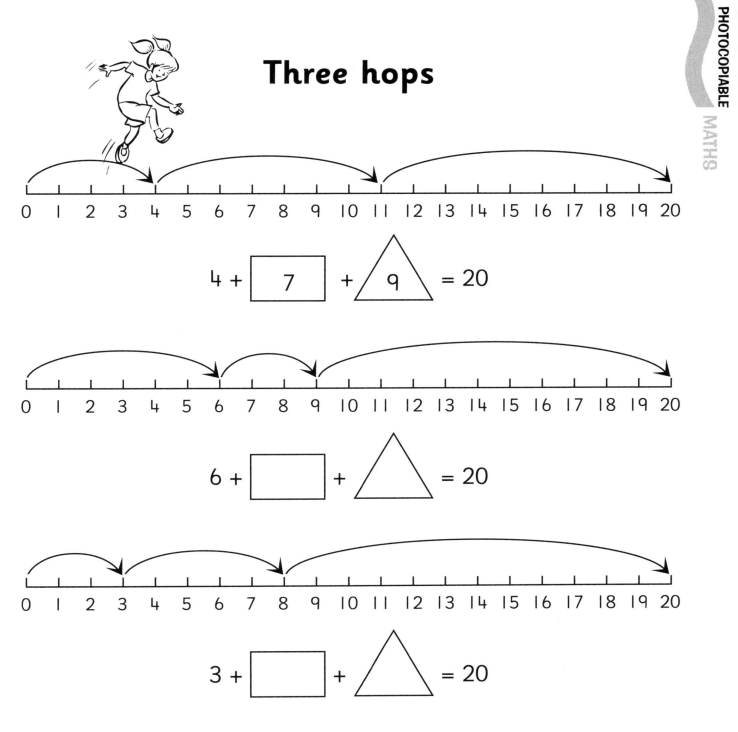

$4 +$ $\boxed{7}$ $+$ $\triangle{9}$ $= 20$

$6 +$ $\boxed{}$ $+$ $\triangle{}$ $= 20$

$3 +$ $\boxed{}$ $+$ $\triangle{}$ $= 20$

How many more sets of three hops to 20 can you make?

___ + ___ ___ = 20

___ + ___ ___ = 20

___ + ___ ___ = 20

___ + ___ ___ = 20

Less than

Fido has fewer spots than Fodo. How many fewer?   _____

What is 3 less than 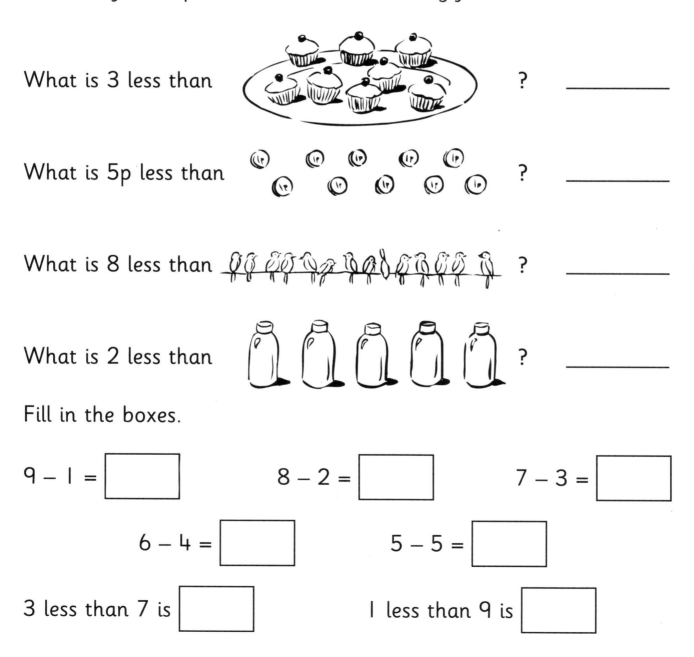 ?   _____

What is 5p less than ?   _____

What is 8 less than ?   _____

What is 2 less than ?   _____

Fill in the boxes.

9 – 1 = ☐   8 – 2 = ☐   7 – 3 = ☐

6 – 4 = ☐   5 – 5 = ☐

3 less than 7 is ☐   1 less than 9 is ☐

Lots of blanks

Fill in the blanks.

2 + 2 + 2 is [3] lots of △ 2

2 + 2 + 2 + 2 is [　] lots of △

5 + 5 is [　] lots of △

5 + 5 + 5 + 5 + 5 + 5 is [　] lots of △

10 + 10 + 10 + 10 is [　] lots of △

10 + 10 + 10 is [　] lots of △

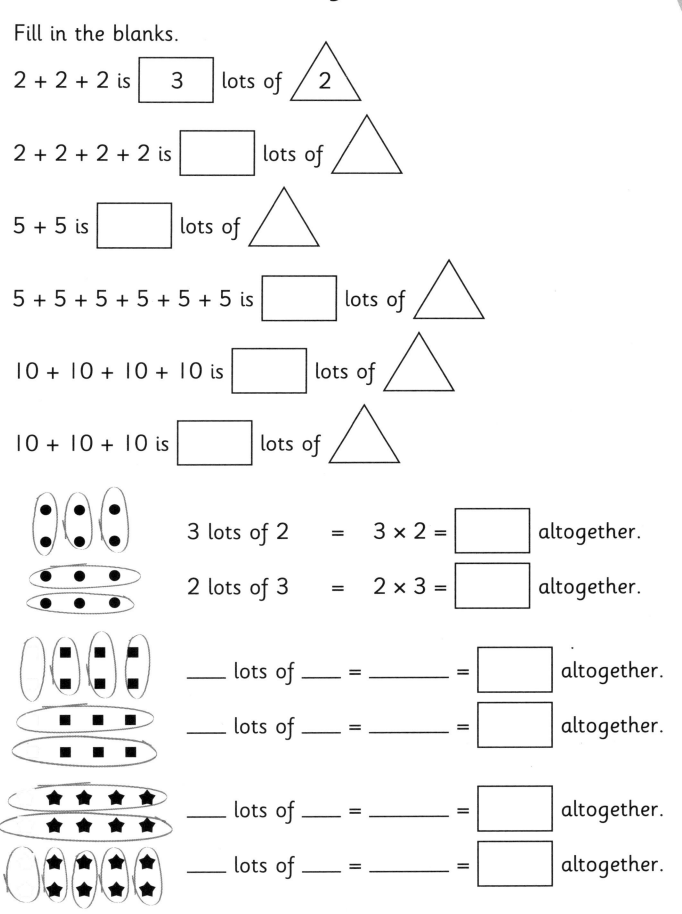

3 lots of 2　　=　3 × 2 = [　] altogether.

2 lots of 3　　=　2 × 3 = [　] altogether.

___ lots of ___ = _____ = [　] altogether.

___ lots of ___ = _____ = [　] altogether.

___ lots of ___ = _____ = [　] altogether.

___ lots of ___ = _____ = [　] altogether.

Sharing equally

Share 8 pound coins equally

between Harry and Sally.

Share 15 apples equally

between Kes, Des and Wes.

Share 8 acorns equally

between Fe, Fi, Fo and Fum.

Share 10 sweets equally

between Sunita, Prianka, Kelly, Esi and Sarabjit.

Halves and doubles

Doubling trail

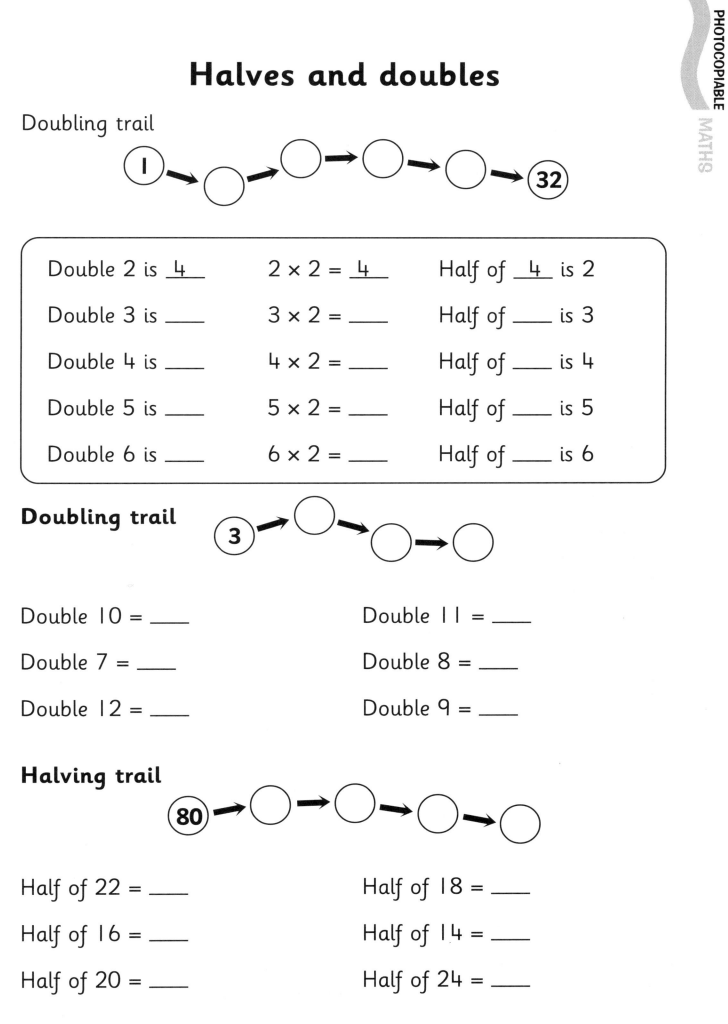

Double 2 is _4_   2 × 2 = _4_   Half of _4_ is 2

Double 3 is ___   3 × 2 = ___   Half of ___ is 3

Double 4 is ___   4 × 2 = ___   Half of ___ is 4

Double 5 is ___   5 × 2 = ___   Half of ___ is 5

Double 6 is ___   6 × 2 = ___   Half of ___ is 6

Doubling trail

Double 10 = ___   Double 11 = ___

Double 7 = ___   Double 8 = ___

Double 12 = ___   Double 9 = ___

Halving trail

Half of 22 = ___   Half of 18 = ___

Half of 16 = ___   Half of 14 = ___

Half of 20 = ___   Half of 24 = ___

The right sign

Write the correct sign (+, −, × or ÷) instead of ★.

7 ★ 4 = 3 ____   21 ★ 9 = 30 ____

25 ★ 7 = 32 ____   12 ★ 2 = 24 ____

10 ★ 2 = 20 ____   100 ★ 2 = 50 ____

80 ★ 2 = 40 ____   5 ★ 2 = 10 ____

64 ★ 5 = 59 ____   17 ★ 5 = 12 ____

Magic squares

1	1	1
2	2	2
3	3	3

→

1	3	2
3	2	1
2	1	3

You can rearrange these numbers so that each column, row and diagonal adds up to the **same** number. Try the same with the numbers below.

4	5	6
4	5	6
4	5	6

→

Problems

Jim and Kim share all these apples equally. Then Jim gives two of his apples to Kim.

How many does Kim have now? _____

How many does Jim have now? _____

8 people are on the bus. 6 get off. 3 get on.

How many are on the bus now? _____

 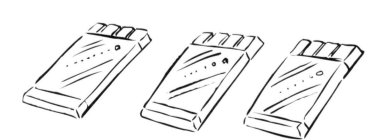

Mac bought 3 chocolate bars for 12p each.

How much change did he get from 50p? _____

Measures

What is the best unit to measure each of these? Connect the pictures to the best unit. You can use some units more than once.

Time to boil an egg

metres

Length of a football pitch

minutes

Weight of a sack of potatoes

litres

Time to fly to Australia

kilograms

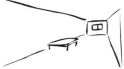

Length of a room

centimetres

Weight of sugar for a cake

grams

Amount of petrol in a car

Length of an envelope

hours

Centimetre lines

Use your ruler to measure these lines. Write down the length of each line in centimetres.

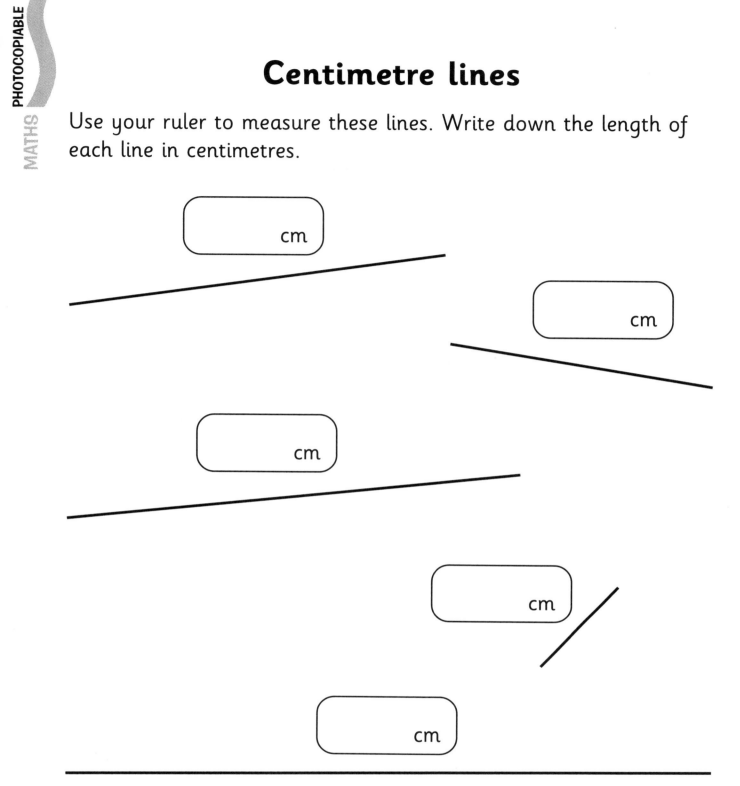

Use your ruler to draw a line that is

11cm long.

8cm long.

On time

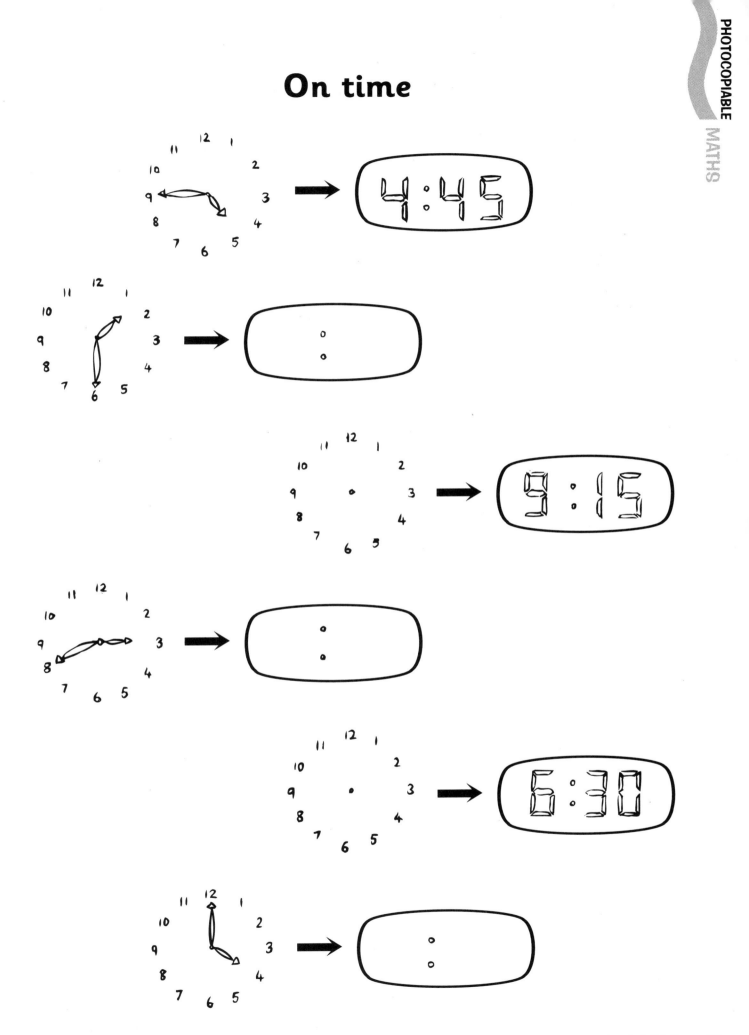

Lines of symmetry

Draw a line of symmetry on each of these shapes.

Complete these symmetrical patterns by colouring.

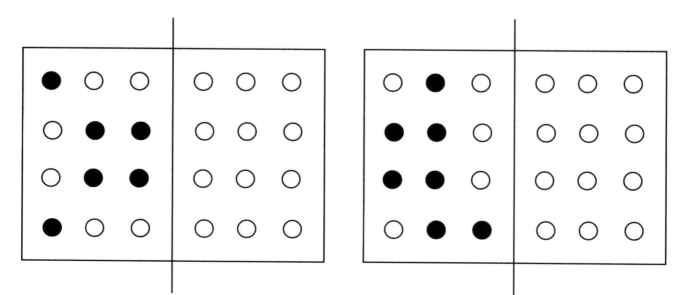

SCIENCE

Because science is based upon observing and experimenting, every sheet in this chapter should be prefaced with a reminder that the children should 'do' before they write. Observation of a real snail is more valuable than examination of a drawing – a notion you should bear in mind throughout this section. For subject matter we have limited ourselves to the QCA Schemes of Work, and within this to those objectives that worksheets are best able to support.

The National Curriculum provides three science 'contexts': Life processes and living things (Sc2), Materials and their properties (Sc3) and Physical processes (Sc4). Scientific enquiry (Sc1) sets out the skills and principles to be taught through these contexts. In Year 2, the QCA scheme covers this ground in six units, allocated a total curriculum time of 51 hours. The units are as follows: 2A Health and growth; 2B Plants and animals in the local environment; 2C Variation; 2D Grouping and changing materials; 2E Forces and movement; 2F Using electricity.

Because of the progressive nature of the scheme, the link between Year 1 and Year 2 units is quite close, and can often be seen from the titles alone. For example, Unit 1E in Year 1 (Pushes and pulls) is followed by Unit 2E in Year 2 (Forces and movement). The worksheets in this chapter, therefore, relate quite closely to the science worksheets in *Year Group Photocopiables: Year 1*. This has the advantage that differentiated work can easily be created, simply by using material prepared for Year 1.

Food on the plate (1) and (2)
(pages 91 and 92)

Objective: To recognise basic food types and to know that humans need food and water to stay alive.

What to do: These two worksheets are intended to be used together. Ask: *What do children eat?* Talk with the class about the different meals they eat, both at home and at school, using the correct vocabulary to describe different food groups (the children should be introduced to the vocabulary listed on the worksheets). Before completing the sheets, it is best to go through the pictures of the foods, perhaps as a class, so that the children are clear as to what each food is. To complete the sheet, the children should simply map each food to the correct plate (category) with a line.

Differentiation: Less able children will need real experience of the foods pictured. Ideally, all children should see and identify these foods, so a visit to the supermarket in small groups, using the sheet as a reference document, is a good idea. (Remember, where real food is involved make sure that all rules of

hygiene are observed – children may be tempted to taste food even when this is not intended.)

Extension: Two main lines of further enquiry are worth pursuing. Get children to analyse the favourite foods of the members of the class and then to present this information as a block graph. Follow up the discussion of food by encouraging children to describe the foods as accurately as possible (by category and taste).

Young and old (page 93)

Objective: To match parents and offspring. To know that animals produce young that grow into adults.

What to do: As they did in Year 1, ask the children to map the pictures of the young to the corresponding picture of an adult by drawing a line. You could ask children to use a different coloured line for each animal.

Differentiation: Work with a group of less able children, and talk about the pictures to make sure that all the animals are correctly identified before they attempt the exercise. Explain that all animals produce young that grow up into adults.

Extension: Talk about ways in which adults differ from their offspring. Ask the children to bring in photographs of people as both child and adult (these could be famous people or members of their family) to make a class display of 'young and old'.

Babies and toddlers (page 94)

Objective: To look at the differences between babies and toddlers, and why they need to be looked after.

What to do: Cut out the pictures at the bottom of the sheet (this may be best carried out by an adult), then ask the children to sort out the pictures according to whether they are something a baby or a toddler can do, sticking them into the space on the sheet once they're happy with their answers.

Differentiation: Where children are not clear about the distinction between a baby and a toddler, draw upon their own experiences at home. A parent with a baby and a toddler could visit the class and answer questions from the children.

Extension: Children could make a list of the differences between babies and toddlers. Ask questions such as: · *When do they go to sleep? What do they eat? How do they move? How do they communicate?*

Is it good for you? (page 95)

Objective: To distinguish between medicines and sweets, and to understand why it is sometimes necessary to take medicines.

What to do: Children *must* understand that medicines are dangerous if taken without the knowledge of parents or doctors. A lot of discussion must precede and follow the completion of this sheet. Children might like to be taken on a high street visit to look at what various shops actually sell. In the first section of the sheet, the children should colour the correct answers in different colours. For the second question, talk with the children about each of the objects listed, and how they know which are medicines. In answer to the final question 'Why do we take medicines?', discuss each of the statements, then ask the children to tick those that are right, and to put a cross against those that are wrong.

Differentiation: You could provide a range of empty medicine containers for the children to examine (take every precaution to keep medicines out of reach of the children). Some children may need reading support for the latter part of the sheet.

Extension: Ask children to say when it is safe for them to take medicines Ask: *Why should we not eat things unless we know what they are?*

Seek and find (page 96)

Objective: To learn that there are different types of plants and animals in the local environment.

What to do: The children should complete this sheet during or after a walk in the locality looking for plants and animals. They can write a list of the names of the creatures that inhabit their local environment. As they complete the sheet, ask the children to write down where they have seen each species of plant or animal ('under a bucket', 'in the long grass'; not 'in Devon'!).

Differentiation: Provide a selection of simple picture reference books for less able children to refer to. Take small groups of children into the school grounds to see how many creatures and plants you can find, completing the sheet 'in the field'.

Extension: Challenge children to choose a familiar local area (perhaps a section of their own garden), and to list any animals and plants that they find there on the worksheet, together with where they found them. Less able children could use the sheet as a kind of checklist, ticking off the animals they find.

Exploring outdoors (page 97)

Objective: To recognise that there are differences between local habitats.

What to do: Explain the worksheet to the children. Together, choose two contrasting local habitats to examine, and ask the children to write the names in the spaces in the tables. The children need to predict what they will find in each habitat, based upon previous experience, writing their ideas in the tables. It is not necessary for a long list to be made. Then, take the children to each of the habitats to record what they find next to their predictions (perhaps using a clipboard). Remember to check the habitats in advance for hazards – dog mess, broken glass and so on, and to observe any LEA guidelines on school visits if these are applicable. Back in the classroom, talk about any differences between the children's guesses and what they actually found.

Differentiation: Some children will need the close support of an adult to carry out this exercise – work with these children in small, supervised groups.

Extension: Collate the children's observational work to make a large class chart showing all the creatures and plants found in the habitats they have looked at. Compare the findings with the children: *What do you find in the playground compared to the long grass?*

Search for seeds (page 98)

Objective: To recognise a variety of seeds from which plants grow.

What to do: The children need to match the pictures of the fruits on the worksheets to the names. When they have done this, ask them to look at the pictures to see if they can spot the seeds from which new plants grow, and to colour the seeds within the fruits.

Differentiation: Provide reference books and, if possible, a display of fruits for less able children.

Extension: Grow some seeds in class (beans or peas are good) and let the children watch their growth.

A for animal, P for plant (page 99)

Objective: To decide whether a familiar living thing is an animal or plant. To give a reason for this decision.

What to do: The children should study the pictures on the worksheet and decide whether each is an animal or a plant, writing *A* for animal or *P* for plant in the box next to each picture. As they complete the activity, talk to the children about how they know which is a plant and which is an animal.

Differentiation: Although it is not necessary to name all the pictures, it may help the less able to do so. Talk to them about what animals have in common (they all move, they have eyes, heads and so on). Use these criteria to sort the pictures into the correct categories: *Can this one move?* (No.) *Then it must be a plant.* Once again, reference books will come in useful.

Extension: Ask the children: *Which group do humans fit into?* Ask for a few simple reasons why humans are animals (we move, we have eyes and so on). Challenge the children to name all the animals and plants on the worksheet by using reference books (perhaps as a homework activity).

The same but different (page 100)

Objective: To learn that humans are similar to each other in some ways and different in others.

What to do: Ask the children to look at the pictures on the worksheet (as well as any other pictures of people you may be able to find), and to think about the ways in which people differ and the ways in which they are the same. They should record their thoughts in the spaces provided, for example 'We all have two eyes and two legs.' and 'Some people have straight hair and others have curly.'

Differentiation: Some children may find the recording a challenge, and they should be helped with the writing. Answers could also be given orally.

Extension: Ask the children to think of ways in which we are different to most other animals (for example, we walk upright on two legs, we don't have fur, we eat using a knife and fork).

How we are different (page 101)

Objective: To understand that there are some differences between children that can be measured.

What to do: Make sure that the children can measure to the nearest whole centimetre before they carry out this activity. They should record their answers on the sheet, having measured Fred's foot against their own. (You could measure the children's shoes rather than the feet.) Encourage the children to talk about other ways in which they are different from one another.

Differentiation: Some children will need help with measuring. It may be best to deal with these children in a small group so that they can be helped and can help each other.

Extension: Measure everyone's feet in the classroom (including the adults if you wish) to the nearest centimetre and make a block graph of the results. You might like to examine other ways in which individuals differ (height, weight, hair length/colour, hand span) and measure and record these as a class.

Natural materials (page 102)

Objective: To identify natural materials and to appreciate that they can be changed in order to make other objects.

What to do: The children should draw a line linking each material on the worksheet to the source material from which it has been manufactured. Once they have completed the sheet, the children should describe how each material has been altered in the space at the bottom of the sheet.

Differentiation: Less able children could give their answers orally rather than in writing. You could ask more able children to think of other objects that might be made from the materials on the sheet.

Extension: Ask children to list six objects from the classroom (or home) that are made from natural materials and to say how the material has been altered.

Heat often changes things (page 103)

Objective: To think about and describe the changes that take place when common materials are heated.

What to do: Note that there are a number of possible answers to some of the questions on the sheet (eggs can be boiled, poached or fried; potatoes can be chipped, baked or mashed and so on). You might like to talk to the children about what happens to each of these things when they are heated and ask the children to think about why they might be heated.

Differentiation: Hands-on experience is the best support for less able children. Ask questions such as: *How would we heat bread (toast)?* As far as is practical, carry out the heating activities that are described on the sheet.

Extension: Make cakes. Help the children mix the ingredients, cook the mixture and observe what happens as it is heated. (Be sure to follow your school's hygiene rules when cooking.)

Forces (page 104)

Objective: To understand that pushes and pulls are examples of forces and to recognise examples of these forces at work.

What to do: When carrying out this activity with the children, make sure you introduce and frequently use the word *forces*, and that the children know what it means. The children should list examples of pushing and pulling forces at work in the spaces on the sheet.

Differentiation: Take a group of less able children and let them try out pushing and pulling activities (pushing a door shut, pulling a PE mat along the floor, for example). Ask them to say whether each action is a push or a pull. When the children have finished, talk about the pictures at the bottom of the sheet. What do they show? More able children could be encouraged to think about objects that are both pushed and pulled.

Extension: Ask: *What happens when we push and pull materials?* Give children a range of materials (such as dough, plasticine, a sponge, rubber balls, rubber bands, a bag of sand, string and so on), and ask them to test what happens when these are pushed and pulled, twisted and squeezed, stretched and manipulated. Classify the actions as pushes or pulls.

Faster and slower (page 105)

Objective: To explain how to make some common things speed up or slow down.

What to do: For each of the three pictures, the children should describe what they would need to do in each case to speed up or slow down. This is a simple exercise if the children have had recent experience of the activity. Try asking questions as they work through the sheet: *How do you go faster or slower on a slide?*

Differentiation: The best support for children who struggle with this sheet is to go out and do each activity (as far as this is practicable) with an adult helping to elicit descriptions from the children as they do each action.

Extension: Choose a piece of apparatus in school (play equipment, for example), and ask the children to think about how they would go faster or slower on it.

Batteries (page 106)

Objective: To learn that some devices use batteries to supply electricity and that these can be used safely.

What to do: Talk about things the children can think of that use electricity. Ask them where these things get their electricity from. Explain the worksheet to the children (point out that the car is radio-controlled). The torch, radio-controlled car, portable cassette player, radio, bike lamp, watch, CD player and portable phone all use batteries.

For the second part of the activity, explain to the children that the 'V' on the battery indicates its 'voltage', and that batteries with a high voltage are stronger than batteries with a low voltage. Make sure the children are aware of the danger of mains electricity, talking about household appliances that are connected to the mains, and which must be used safely. Show the children examples of how these are used safely in school.

Differentiation: Display a range of battery- and mains-powered appliances. Take some of the batteries out to show the children what they are like – this supports children with hands-on experience.

Extension: Ask children to write a list of battery-powered objects that they have at home. Which uses the most powerful batteries?

Bulbs and circuits (page 107)

Objective: To recognise drawings of simple circuits. To be able to explain whether they will work or not.

What to do: Provide the equipment shown on the sheet. It need not be exactly the same, comparable bulbs and batteries will do equally well. To avoid frustration, test the equipment before the activity, making sure that connections work, the batteries are not flat and so on. Make sure that bulbs and batteries are compatible, because batteries that are too strong can burn out bulbs. (Match a 1.5V battery to a 1.5V bulb; a 6V battery to a 6.5V bulb and so on.)

Give the children plenty of time to experiment with the wires and batteries (batteries of this voltage are quite safe), creating the circuits as shown on the sheet. The children should state on the sheet whether each arrangement will light the bulb. As they do so, ask them why they think this is the case.

Differentiation: Allow plenty of time for slower children to experiment, finding out for themselves what happens when each circuit is built. Do not rush in with prepared answers! More able children could try building other circuits using the equipment, although under close supervision.

Extension: Provide different equipment for the children to try (use a buzzer instead of a bulb, for example).

Two bulbs (page 108)

Objective: To make a complete circuit that will operate two bulbs successfully.

What to do: Provide the equipment listed on the sheet and let the children try to build a circuit as instructed there. As in the previous activity, make sure that the bulbs and batteries are matched. There is more than one way of making both bulbs light up (by setting the bulbs up in series (in a row) or in parallel (in two separate loops), but this does not matter at this stage. Once they have a complete circuit, they should draw it in the space on the sheet. Any recognisable picture of the circuit drawn by the children is acceptable.

Differentiation: Some children will need more time than others to create their circuits. Provide as much time as is needed; there are no short cuts so let the children complete this activity for themselves. Let the children experiment – give them time, not answers. Ask: *Does anybody know where the electricity flows?*

Extension: Challenge children to add an extra bulb to the circuit.

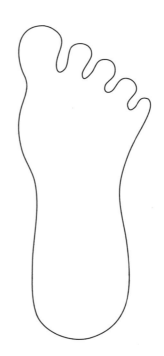

Food on the plate (1)

cabbage

naan bread

broccoli

ciabatta

vegetables

grapes

beansprouts

fruit

carrots

pear

bread

apples

baguette

strawberries

pitta bread

Food on the plate (2)

steak

cannelloni

farfalle

spaghetti

meat

chicken

ham

made from milk

butter

cheddar

pasta

gouda

cream

sausages

ravioli

Young and old

Draw lines to match the young with their adult.

Babies and toddlers

How do babies and toddlers eat? How do they drink? How do they move? Cut out the pictures and sort them out.

Baby   **Toddler**

Talk about the differences.

Is it good for you?

Where do we get medicines from? Where do we get sweets from?

Chemist · Pharmacy · Newsagent · Bank · Supermarket · Village store · Doctor

We should never eat medicines unless we are told it is safe. Circle the medicines below.

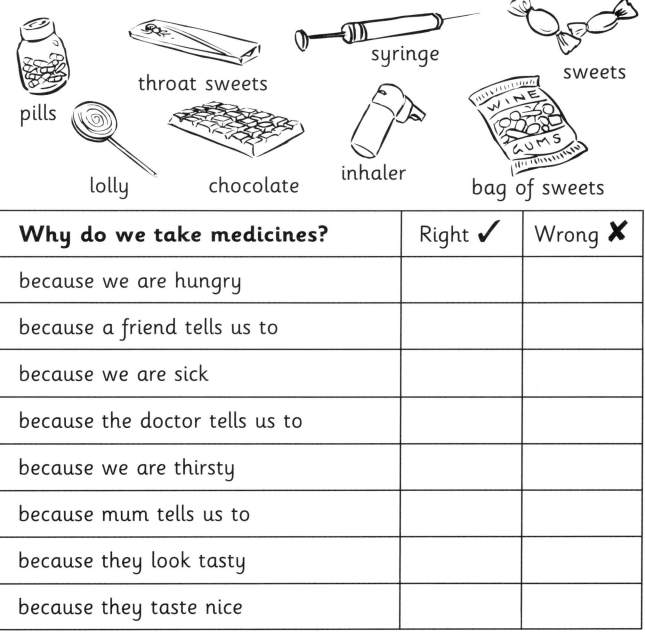

pills · throat sweets · syringe · sweets · lolly · chocolate · inhaler · bag of sweets

Why do we take medicines?	Right ✔	Wrong ✘
because we are hungry		
because a friend tells us to		
because we are sick		
because the doctor tells us to		
because we are thirsty		
because mum tells us to		
because they look tasty		
because they taste nice		

Seek and find

What are these?

Can you find any of these? Where do you find them?

I found _____

_____

_____

_____

Exploring outdoors

Choose two different places close to the school where there are different plants and animals. You could choose:

a shady area

some tall grass

a pond

a damp wall

My chosen places are:

1. _____	
Animals and plants I expect to find there.	What I found there when I looked.

2. _____	
Animals and plants I expect to find there.	What I found there when I looked.

How good were your guesses?
Explain the differences between the habitats.

Search for seeds

Which plants do these fruits come from?

grapes   pear   apple   orange   tomato   sunflower

Can you see the seeds in each of the fruits? Colour the seeds.

A for animal, P for plant

Which of these are plants? Which are animals? Write **P** next to the plants, and **A** next to the animals.

Write down one difference between plants and animals.

_____

The same but different

These people are all different, but they are the same in some ways.

They are the same because _____

_____

_____

_____

_____

They are different because _____

_____

_____

_____

_____

How we are different

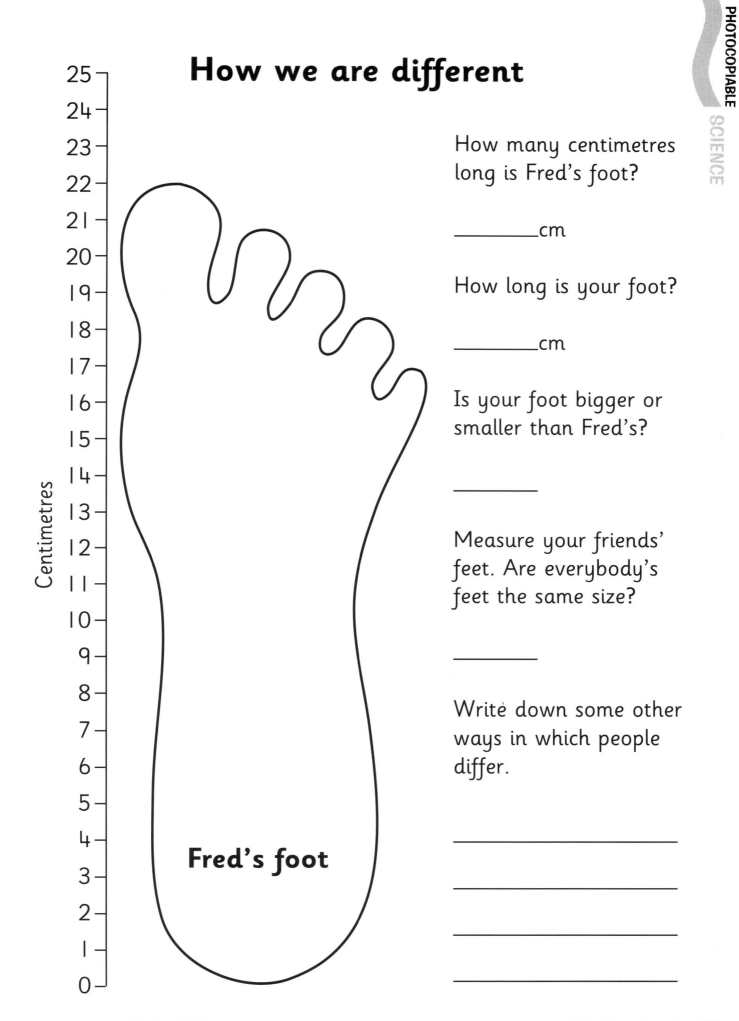

Centimetres

25
24
23
22
21
20
19
18
17
16
15
14
13
12
11
10
9
8
7
6
5
4
3
2
1
0

Fred's foot

How many centimetres long is Fred's foot?

_____cm

How long is your foot?

_____cm

Is your foot bigger or smaller than Fred's?

_____

Measure your friends' feet. Are everybody's feet the same size?

_____

Write down some other ways in which people differ.

_____

_____

_____

_____

Natural materials

Link each object to the material it is made from.

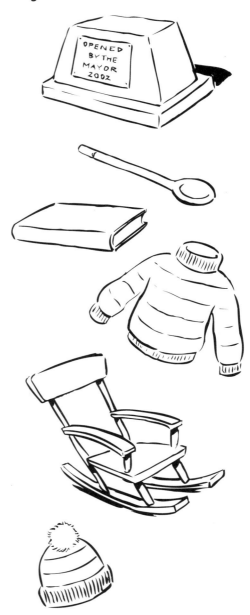

What has happened to the material?

_____

_____

_____

_____

Heat often changes things

Draw what each of these things might be like after heating. Write down why you think we might heat them.

Forces

pushing

pulling

Pushes and pulls are examples of **forces**.

Make a list of things moved by:

pushing	pulling

Faster and slower

	How to go faster	How to go slower

Batteries

Batteries provide electricity. Which of these objects use batteries to make them work? Circle those that use batteries.

> **WARNING:**
> Mains electricity can be very dangerous. It can kill!!

Here are some batteries. Which is the most powerful? How can you tell?

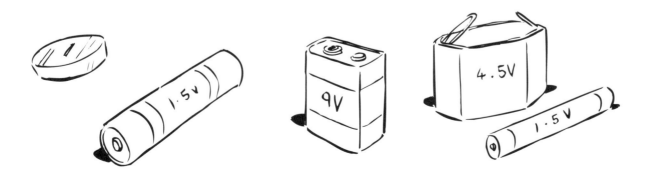

Bulbs and circuits

Make these circuits.
You will need wires, batteries, bulbs, tape and a screwdriver.

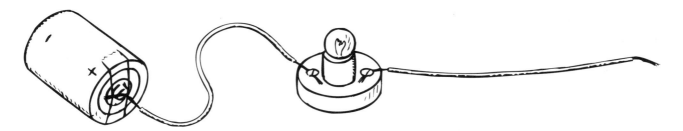

Will this bulb light? _____

Will this bulb light? _____

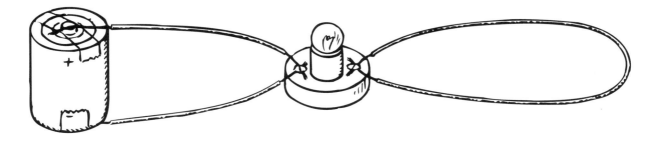

Will this bulb light? _____

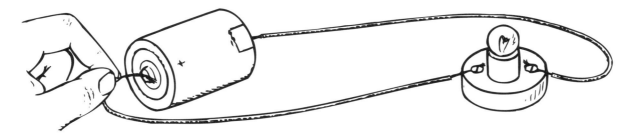

Will this bulb light? _____

Two bulbs

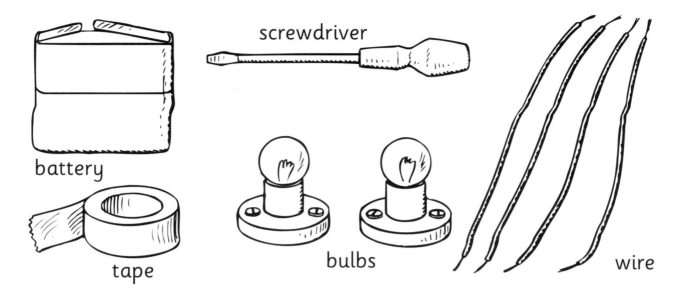

battery

screwdriver

tape

bulbs

wire

Find a way of making both bulbs light up at the same time.
Draw your circuit here.

HISTORY

Although it is not possible at any stage to acquire knowledge, skills and understanding in history without hanging them on the peg of content, at Key Stage 1 the required content is defined only in general terms. So, while the Programme of Study specifies that children should be taught 'past events from the history of Britain and the wider world', it does not direct teachers to a defined canon of events. Nevertheless, we do still have to choose people and events to focus on, and Year 2 is the time to do it.

The QCA scheme homes in on one loosely defined area of study (seaside holidays in the past), one particular historical character from British history (Florence Nightingale) and one event (the Great Fire of London). These are good historical choices, and we have focused on them in this section in order to support teachers using the scheme. But they are not the only possible choices; one could equally justify studying, for example, going to school in the past, Isambard Kingdom Brunel and the Gunpowder Plot. The decision is yours, but you should ensure that you refer to the Breadth of Study section in the National Curriculum for guidance in choosing.

These worksheets are intended to support work on these QCA-recommended topics, not to introduce them, so they should be used with the children alongside other teaching resources.

Postcards from the seaside (1), (2) and (3) (pages 112–114)

Objective: To find out about holidays in the past from photographs. To sequence photographs in chronological order, giving reasons for choosing that particular order.

What to do: These three worksheets are part of the same activity. Cut out the postcards from each worksheet and mount them on card so that they will withstand handling.

The children should work in groups (you can decide on the most appropriate size), thinking and talking about what seaside holidays might have been like in the past compared with today. Ask them to look at the pictures on the postcards, noting similarities and differences in what they can see. Look at the two modern pictures: *How can you tell these are from the present day? Is there anything familiar about the pictures?* Ask the children to choose the pictures they think are the oldest, taken before most grown-ups were born – why do they think these are the oldest? What about the two that remain? (These might represent Granddad's or even Great-granddad's holidays.)

Talk about time order, and what we might expect to see in pictures taken a long time ago that we wouldn't expect to see today. Display the pictures (copies could be stuck into books) in three clear periods – a long time ago, when Gran and Granddad were young, and today.

Differentiation: There is a lot to find in these worksheets, and even the less able will be able to make a contribution to the discussion and to the detective work. This is best aided by minimal (or at least not over-eager) adult intervention and by creating mixed-ability groups for the children to work in.

Extension: Ask children to look for similar pictures or objects at home (perhaps an old holiday postcard, or Granddad's old swimsuit). Encourage the children to talk about these items, explaining how they can tell which 'period' they belong to. Add them to a class display about holidays. This work can be linked to geography, especially the QCA unit on the seaside.

Who was Florence Nightingale? (page 115)

Objective: To learn and order events in the life of Florence Nightingale.

What to do: Tell the children the story of Florence Nightingale. You might simply recount the details given on the worksheet, or read from a biography of Florence. Try to get the facts established in the children's minds, and ask them questions such as: *Why do you think that she was named 'Florence'?* (She was born there.) *Why did she go abroad to train? Why did she return to Britain to raise money to train nurses?* (Soon after her arrival in the Crimea, her 38 nurses were tending 10 000 sick and wounded following the Battle of Inkerman.) Ask the children to cut out the pictures on the worksheet, and to put the pictures telling the story of her life into the right order. Having decided on the correct order, they should stick the pictures in their books or on another sheet of paper.

Differentiation: Some children may be able to complete this sheet alone, but most will need to work co-operatively to get the most out of this exercise. Provide reading support where needed.

Extension: Ask children to tell the story of Florence Nightingale in their own words. A group could act out the story of her life, or an episode from it (such as when more and more wounded kept arriving at the hospital in Scutari when it was already overcrowded). What might they do? What do they think that Florence did?

This is Florence Nightingale (page 116)

Objective: To recognise a famous person from the past; to identify similarities and differences between what people wore then and what people wear today.

What to do: This, and the following worksheet, is intended to support work on Florence Nightingale. Talk with the children about what we mean by a 'famous person'. Look at the picture of Florence Nightingale on the worksheet, and ask the children, in pairs or small groups, to answer the questions on the sheet. The pictures could be cut out and stuck into books where

children could note the similarities and differences between Florence Nightingale and a modern-day nurse.

Differentiation: Children will benefit from working in groups of mixed ability. Make sure that there are plenty of reference books to hand for the children to use, showing not only Victorian Times but also modern nursing.

Extension: Ask the children: *Why was Florence Nightingale famous?* Children may not appreciate how difficult it was for someone, particularly a woman, to do what Florence Nightingale did. Provide pictures for the children to look at as you talk about Florence Nightingale's work, particularly her work in the Crimea, and try to create some understanding of the distances involved in travelling to the Crimea. Nightingale's contribution to the nursing of the sick and wounded in the Crimea is well known, although some questions have been raised about how effective her work was. She was, however, instrumental in revolutionising nursing in Britain. She started training schools at St Thomas' and King's College hospitals in London. Her book *Notes on Nursing* went though many editions, and she was hugely influential on medical matters throughout her life.

Scutari hospital (page 117)

Objective: To think about what life would have been like in the hospital at Scutari when Florence Nightingale was alive.

What to do: Divide the class into groups. Ask them to study the picture of Florence Nightingale in Scutari hospital on the worksheet, and to write down four things they can learn from the picture about what life was like in the Scutari hospital when Florence Nightingale was caring for the sick there. Once each group has made a list, ask the children to discuss and agree on what is the most important thing they have learned from the picture, and to underline that sentence. Discuss these choices as a class, and ask the children for simple explanations of their choices.

Differentiation: More able children need not be limited in the number of things they note from the picture. Less able children might concentrate on choosing two things that they can learn from the picture.

Extension: Allow children to look at as many books, pictures and other sources on the period that

© The London Illustrated News

you have to hand. In pairs, ask children to list all the facts about Florence, the Scutari hospital and the Crimean War that they can find. Limit the time available for the exercise, and at the end ask pairs to share their facts with the rest of the class.

The Great Fire: where and when?
(page 118)

Objective: To locate the Great Fire of London in time and place.

What to do: This worksheet helps to set the Great Fire of London in a historical context, and could also be used as an introduction to the event as a topic. The children can bring their wider knowledge to bear on a subject such as this (for example, a previous visit to London, or programmes seen on television). Let the children work in pairs or small groups to tackle this sheet, and allow them time to reach conclusions about the pictures. Answers can be either in a written form or given orally. As a class, talk with the children about how they can tell which pictures belong together.

Differentiation: Vary the amount of time you allocate to groups. Be patient; provide reference books to support children if necessary, but not too readily.

Extension: Create a simple class timeline and mark the location of both pictures on it. Encourage the children to add to the timeline as they learn about other events and periods. If the chart is located at eye-level in the classroom, the children can order events on the timeline as a practical exercise.

The story of the Great Fire (page 119)

Objective: To sequence the events of the Great Fire correctly.

What to do: Tell the children the story of the Great Fire. Base your account on information from reference books, but dramatise the story, adding as much detail as you feel necessary. After hearing the story, ask the children to cut the cartoon pictures out from the worksheet, and to rearrange them in the correct order. The children could use the pictures as part of a more complete story of the Great Fire, with the pictures coloured in and mounted in books.

Differentiation: Provide picture reference books for those that need support, and adult reading support for less confident children.

Extension: Ask the children to draw further pictures of the Great Fire based on the facts they have learned in the lesson. They should add a suitable caption, and add the pictures to the story sequence.

An eyewitness (page 120)

Objective: To understand what an eyewitness is; to know that Samuel Pepys saw the Great Fire and wrote about it in his diary.

What to do: This sheet is about evidence, both pictorial and written. Ask the children: *How do we know about any fire?* Explain the ways in which we know about the Great Fire of London (eyewitness accounts, government reports, paintings or archaeological evidence, for example). Read the extracts from Samuel Pepys' diary on the worksheet – the language will be unfamiliar to the children, but alter the extracts only where really necessary. Let the children choose one of the extracts on the sheet and ask them to draw a small illustration of it. Compare the pictures and challenge them to say why each one is different.

Differentiation: Using documentary evidence is difficult with very young children, but history is a literary subject and it's surprising what children can deduce even from a complex text – provide help only when necessary. Some will find this sheet very difficult, in which case it can simply accompany an oral lesson. You might also concentrate on the evidence that can be drawn from the picture.

Extension: Challenge children to find out some facts about Samuel Pepys (perhaps as homework). You might like to ask children to report on an incident that they all saw, and then compare their eyewitness accounts. Try staging an incident in the playground using older children or adults (without the class's knowledge) and challenge children to report on it afterwards. How reliable are the eyewitnesses?

Postcards from the seaside (1)

We are having an awfully jolly time in
BROADSTAIRS

Postcards from the seaside (2)

SCHOLASTIC **113**

Postcards from the seaside (3)

© Corel

© Corel

Who was Florence Nightingale?

Cut out these pictures of events in Florence Nightingale's life.
Put them in the right order.

She trained as a nurse in Germany and France.

She saw that dirty hospitals caused death.

She was born in 1820 in Florence.

She raised money to train nurses.

During the war with Russia, she went with 38 nurses to help the wounded soldiers.

She wrote an important book called *Notes on Nursing.*

This is Florence Nightingale

Look at these pictures. Which one do you think is a picture of

Florence Nightingale?

How can you tell? _____

What work might these people do? _____

Compare their clothes.

Scutari hospital

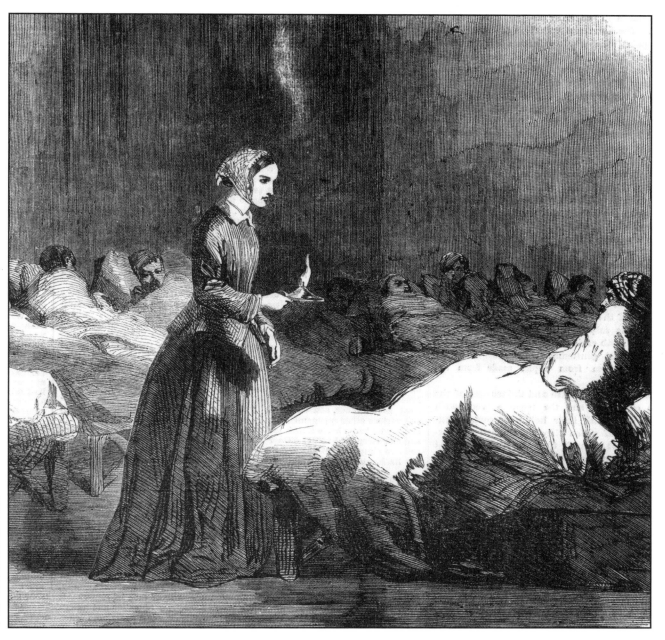

What was it like in Scutari hospital?
Write down what you can tell from the picture.

_____

_____

_____

_____

The Great Fire: where and when?

Where is this?
How can you tell?

© Photodisc, Inc.

Which picture does each man belong to?
Draw a line connecting the person to the correct picture.

The story of the Great Fire

Cut out these pictures and put them in the right order.

The fire spread rapidly, because it was hot and the wooden houses were dry.

The fire was controlled by blowing up houses with gunpowder so it had nothing more to burn.

The fire started in Pudding Lane.

The firefighters had only leather buckets and a few simple fire engines.

An eyewitness

How do we know what happened in the Great Fire of London?
Samuel Pepys kept a diary.

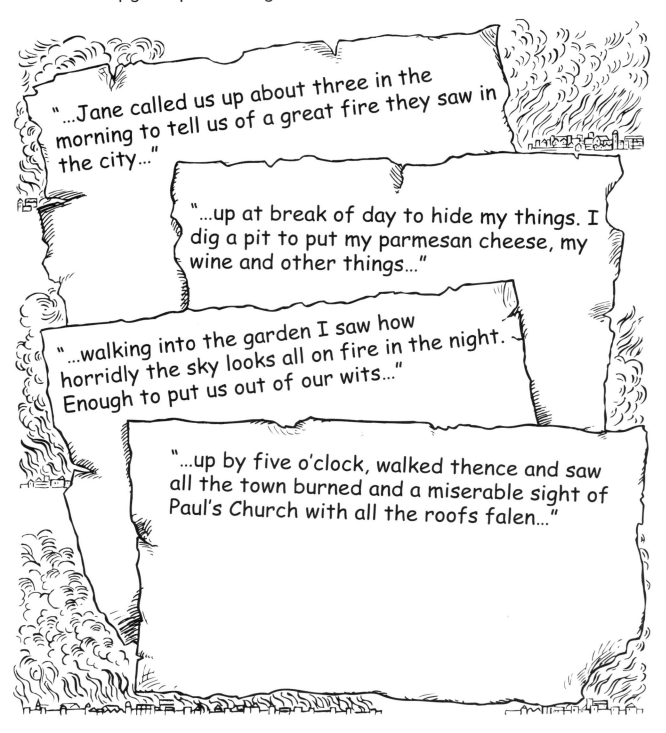

"...Jane called us up about three in the morning to tell us of a great fire they saw in the city..."

"...up at break of day to hide my things. I dig a pit to put my parmesan cheese, my wine and other things..."

"...walking into the garden I saw how horridly the sky looks all on fire in the night. Enough to put us out of our wits..."

"...up by five o'clock, walked thence and saw all the town burned and a miserable sight of Paul's Church with all the roofs falen..."

What is an eyewitness?

GEOGRAPHY

National curriculum geography for infants is nothing if not interesting and varied. Once again, the QCA Schemes of Work have been used as the underlying influence on the worksheets in this section, and we have been particularly careful in choosing to support the main thrust of the national curriculum as well as of the QCA schemes. We have targeted work on the seaside and holiday travel, both subjects covered in QCA units for Year 2. Because the only way to Struay is on a flight of fancy, we have chosen to keep our feet on the ground and have excluded it from our choices. The choice of 'a contrasting locality overseas' to study is open, and will be subject to wide local variation, so for obvious reasons that too has been excluded from this section.

It is difficult to calculate the amount of time that might be spent on geography in Year 2, largely because geographical work is likely to become enmeshed with work in other subject areas (the seaside study fits well with historical work, for example). Using the QCA estimates as a starting point, geography would probably consume about 18 hours of curriculum time in Year 2.

Who's been on holiday? (page 123)

Objective: To name possible holiday destinations; to organise a survey.

What to do: Talk with the children about holidays, and about places that they have visited (this may require sensitive handling to ensure that children are not excluded from the discussion). Using the table on the worksheet, ask the children to carry out a survey of places visited by their classmates, colouring in the squares on the worksheet as each child makes their selection (choosing the last place they went to on holiday). Talk with the class about the findings of the survey and look for each of the locations on a map of the world.

Differentiation: Use travel brochures to jog the memory of those that need support: show them pictures of the places and talk with them about their holiday experiences. This sheet will be easier if holidays are fresh in children's minds – the beginning of the autumn term. More able children could plan a more in-depth survey looking at the 'other locations' that children have visited.

Extension: Display atlases, world maps and globes for the children to use; challenge them to find their holiday destination on one of these. For homework, you might ask the children to prepare a short talk (illustrated with artefacts and pictures) about their holiday.

Country, town and seaside
(page 124)

Objective: To identify places and relate them to different types of environments.

What to do: Completion of this worksheet requires a similar strategy to the previous activity, but should be preceded by a discussion of what we mean by 'country', 'town' and 'seaside'. There may be some overlap between the categories to discuss (Blackpool could be 'Town' or 'Seaside', for example) – children should decide on the defining characteristic of the location. Ask them to consider which category their most recent holiday destination fits into, then carry out the survey. (Although this and the preceding worksheet have a different focus, you may choose to do only one of the two, or use both as part of the same survey.)

Differentiation: For those children who do not fully understand the nature of the categories, you might like to set them to work in a mixed-ability group on this task.

Extension: Make a class display illustrating different holiday destinations. Ask each child to contribute something to the display, then challenge the class to identify the category that each destination fits into.

The beach (page 125)

Objective: To identify the physical features associated with a seaside holiday place.

What to do: If possible, this worksheet should be enlarged to A3 and the labels should be cut out ready for the children to use. Look at the picture with the children and allow them to enjoy colouring it in, adding people and animals to it and so on. Give each child a set of labels and ask them to label the parts of the picture accordingly. They can be stuck on, although you may wish to use Blu-Tack or similar so that the labels can be moved about easily.

Differentiation: Children will need to be able to read and understand the labels on the sheet before completing the activity, so they should not undertake this exercise without preliminary work. The sheet could be made into an OHP transparency and used as the focus for a whole-class session before the individual work, for example. Even so, less able children may need the support of an adult to help with the reading of the labels.

Extension: Ask the children to look at a map to find the nearest seaside place to the school. Ask: *Has anybody been there? What is it like? Does it have any of the features in the picture?*

The seaside 150 years ago

(page 126)

Objective: To identify features of a holiday at the seaside in the past.

What to do: The drawing on this worksheet is based upon a famous picture of Ramsgate Sands painted in 1854. You may prefer to enlarge the picture to A3 size (it can also be linked to work in the history section). Use the picture initially for group discussion, asking the children to find out as much information from it as they can. The children can link the words at the bottom of the page to the picture using pencil lines. The storytelling activity can be done orally or in simple written sentences. You might like to prompt the children's stories with questions: *Who is this person? How is he or she dressed? Where did he or she come from? Why is he there? How did she get to the seaside? What is he doing? What do you think he or she will be doing next?*

Differentiation: Less able children could concentrate on discussion of the picture and matching the words to the picture.

Extension: Make 'then' and 'now' lists, comparing the picture to the seaside today. What is different? What is the same?

Travel brochure (page 127)

Objective: To use secondary sources to find out information; to develop awareness of the wider world.

What to do: This activity works best if used alongside brochures from travel agents and geographical reference books. Divide the children into groups and let them tackle the sheet as a puzzle. Ask: *Which name matches each picture?* (One link is done for them.) Give the children time; they should use their own knowledge and the reference materials available to reach decisions that are reasonable. The places have been chosen to be widely different – use a globe to help the children find the places on the sheet (they may need help).

Differentiation: The support of a mixed-ability group should help all children to complete the task.

Extension: Ask each child to choose one of the places on the worksheet, and to write a report for a travel brochure about that place for homework.

Going on holiday (page 128)

Objective: To describe what different places are like; to recognise that places are affected by the weather.

What to do: This sheet fits the objectives of both the National Curriculum and a number of units in the QCA Scheme of Work. It is also useful if you are using the 'Barnaby Bear' approach. The children should match each of the cuddly characters to the place for which they are most appropriately dressed, based upon examination of their attire. You may like the children to cut out all the pictures and reassemble them in the correct pairings on another sheet of paper or in a book. Ask the children to tell you what makes each place different. How do they know where to place the bear?

Differentiation: Less able children could work on this task in small groups.

Extension: Choose one picture, and ask the children to pack an imaginary suitcase, listing everything they would need to go to that place for a holiday.

Who's been on holiday?

Ask your friends where they went for their last holiday.
Colour one square for each friend who has visited that place.

America									
Britain									
France									
Greece									
Spain									
Other place									

Which is the most popular holiday destination? _____

Can you find each of these places on a map?

Country, town and seaside

Ask your class where they stayed on a holiday.
What sort of place was it?

Which is the most popular? Why?

The beach

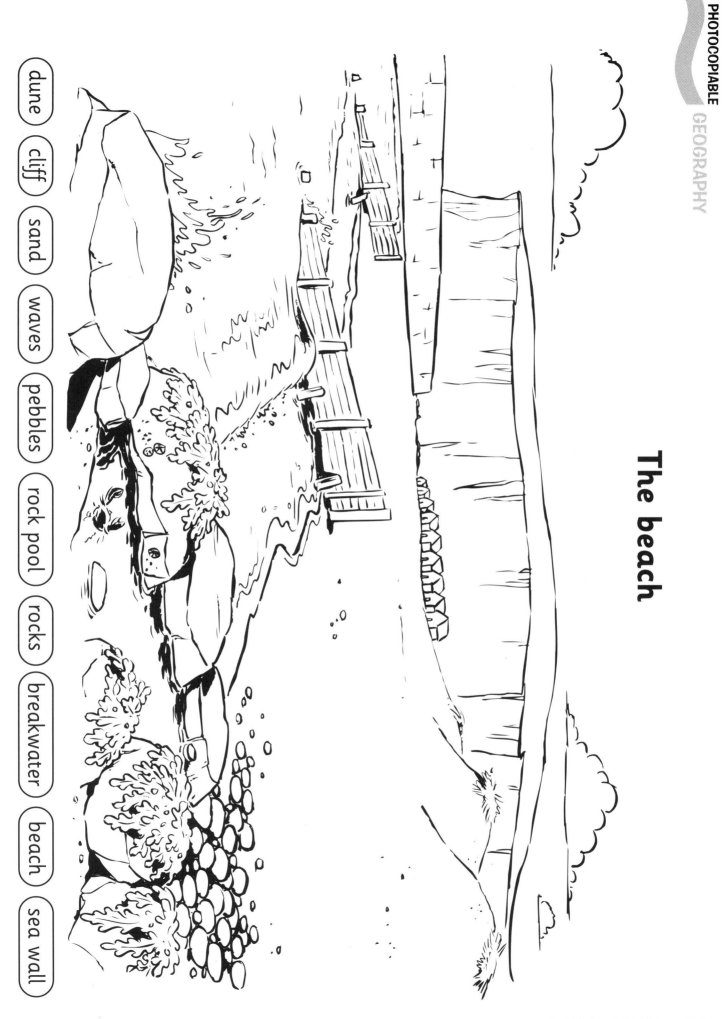

dune · cliff · sand · waves · pebbles · rock pool · rocks · breakwater · beach · sea wall

The seaside 150 years ago

Tell a story about one of the people in the picture.
How is this beach different from a beach you have been to?

(bonnet) (waves) (cliffs) (parasol) (beach)

(sand) (Punch and Judy) (paddling) (telescope)

Travel brochure

Use books and travel brochures to match the pictures to the places.

Sydney, Australia

Blackpool, England

Florida, America

Costa del Sol, Spain

Hong Kong, China

Find each of these places on a map.

Going on holiday

Who's going where?

DESIGN AND TECHNOLOGY

When the National Curriculum went through its first major revision, design and technology went through very little change, which has meant that schools' schemes of work, and those devised by the QCA itself, have undergone little alteration. The word 'disassemble' has been removed from the original scheme, but children are still expected to look at how products have been made and put together.

More than anything, design and technology in the National Curriculum is concerned with *developing ideas* – that is, planning, making products and evaluating them. This can be done by investigating familiar products, through practical tasks (for developing skills and techniques), and by designing and making products. Practical experience is the key to all learning at Key Stage 1, but particularly in design and technology. This is time-consuming, and it is worth noting that the QCA Scheme of Work for Year 2 allocates 29–37 hours of teaching. The scheme is in four units: two focused on mechanisms and structures, and two on textiles. The units are, in fact, very specific projects – there is one on the Biblical story of Joseph's coat of many colours – but we have tried to support these, and other projects you might carry out in Year 2, by concentrating on general elements of a project, and on those activities where the use of a photocopiable worksheet is appropriate.

Tractor (page 131)

Objective: To look at a vehicle, identifying and labelling key parts; to use this information to inform their own design ideas.

What to do: Let the children look at this picture in their own time, as it is intended to inform the design of a vehicle they will make themselves. The children should connect the labels to the correct parts of the vehicle. You may like to ask them to add a driver, colour the picture or add a trailer. Alternatively, enlarge the picture to A3, cut out the tractor and mount it on a 'field' background with the labels stuck on.

Differentiation: Provide plenty of reference books as support; model tractors to handle and examine would also be useful. Less able children might carry this out as a co-operative task.

Extension: Ask the children to design and make a wheeled vehicle for a set purpose. Talk about the purpose first, then think about the features such a vehicle will need (number of wheels and so on). Ask: *What materials will you need?* (Full details of how to approach a design and build project like this are given in Unit 2A of the QCA Scheme of Work for design and technology.)

Vehicles with a purpose (page 132)

Objective: To recognise that there are many different types of vehicle made for many different purposes.

What to do: The children need to be able to identify wheels and axles on a vehicle before this activity, so complementing the previous worksheet. Children should identify and name the vehicles on the worksheet, describe the purpose for which it was made, and record the number of wheels and axles they think the vehicle has. Draw attention to the steering wheel and spare wheels that some vehicles have and talk with the children about whether these should be included (you may prefer to exclude them from the count and stick to wheels that make contact with the ground). The vehicles on the sheet are: an ambulance, a shopping trolley, a pushchair (three wheels), a fire engine, a multi-axled juggernaut, a military jeep, a caravan (one axle) and a small family car.

Differentiation: Hands-on experience is the best form of differentiation – model vehicles are an excellent way of working out how many wheels a vehicle has (and are better than playing with real traffic!). You may wish to spend time with groups of children observing vehicles that drive past the school. A tour of 'teacher's car' is useful, but make sure that this is done in a place of safety. Provide cards with the names of the vehicles on to assist the less able.

Extension: Ask children to make simple freehand drawings of a vehicle of their choice, naming it and labelling its key parts (you might like to exclude the vehicles on the sheet). This could be a homework task.

Hands up! (page 133)

Objective: To identify parts of a puppet; to use a template to make a puppet.

What to do: There are two elements to this sheet: first, understanding what a hand puppet is and how it works; then using the template provided on the worksheet as the basis for making a simple hand puppet. The first part involves preliminary work: talk with the children about puppet shows they have seen, and look at the pictures on the sheet. You could show videos of a puppet show, or bring in some real puppets for the children to see. The second, practical, part allows the children to design and make a puppet of their own. As they do this, ask questions: *What features are you going to give your puppet? Is it a one eyed pirate? A fairy? A professor with spectacles?* Provide fabric and collage materials for the children to use when cutting out and adapting the basic template on the worksheet. The materials used to make the puppets, and the amount of support for this activity, will depend upon the skills and experience of the children. Ideally, the children should cut their designs from non-fraying material, and use needle and thread for joining the front and back of the puppet.

Differentiation: Adult support is the key for less able children. The two pieces of material can be joined by gluing if desired.

Extension: Children could plan and act out a story using the puppets they have made. You might wish to ask children to consider ways of making more complicated, more sophisticated, puppets with separate heads.

Wind-up action (page 134)

Objective: To learn how a winding mechanism works.

What to do: Show the children a selection of toys that have simple winding mechanisms, such as cranes or toy cars. Look at the pictures on the sheet, and discuss the names for the parts of the mechanism. Ask the children to link the labels on the sheet to the appropriate parts of the pictures, and then to talk about how each of the objects work.

Differentiation: Most technology work can be differentiated by the degree of adult support provided – some children will simply need more adult support than others.

Extension: Designing and building a wind-up mechanism is really the next step, which is covered in the next activity. Children could list any winding mechanisms that they come across at home over a period of, say, a week.

Hickory Dickory Dock
(page 135)

Objective: To design and construct a simple winding mechanism that works.

What to do: This worksheet follows on from the previous one. Recite (and if necessary, learn) the words to 'Hickory Dickory Dock' with the children, then explain that they are going to make a working model of the rhyme – the mouse must run up the clock. The diagram on the worksheet shows how to set this activity up and what you will need to provide the children with. Discuss how the children could use what they have learned about wind-up

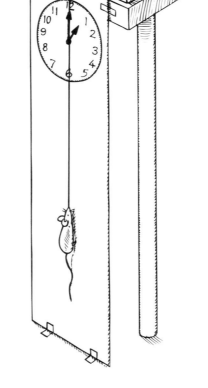

mechanisms to make the mouse move. Examine the pictures on the worksheet and ask the children questions: *What could you use for axles? Where will they go? What about the handle for winding? What might be a good way of making the mouse?* In small groups, the children should work together to make the mechanism. Don't forget to give instructions about the safe use of tools.

Differentiation: All children should work in groups, but some will need constant adult supervision and support, but try not to intervene too much. Getting the axle in the winding gear parallel to the one at the top of the clock is a tricky problem, and may need help.

Extension: Ask children to identify the weak points of their design. Ask: *What could you do to improve it?*

A fishy business (page 136)

Objective: To examine and design repeated patterns. To turn a 2-D design into a 3-D object using paper templates and simple joining techniques.

What to do: The children need to see examples of repeating pattern designs on fabrics, wallpaper and so on to help them with this activity. Ask them to look at the repeating designs on the worksheet. Ask: *Can you copy them using sticky paper? Crayons?*

Using two copies of the worksheet, ask the children to try out one of their repeating patterns on the fish, colouring in opposite sides so that they can be joined by gluing the edges together. They can give the fish substance by filling the inside with cotton wool or similar, before using the fish shape as a template to execute their design using fabrics, sewing the parts together and using other fabrics to create the patterns.

Differentiation: Show children pictures of tropical fish, and look at the colours and shapes to provide inspiration. Provide adult help for less able children in the 'designing and making' stage.

Extension: Provide an outline of a fish on a computer paint package (such as *Microsoft Paint*), and ask the children to paint a design using the 'Fill', 'Spray' and 'Line' tools. Print the children's work out and display them alongside the 3-D fish.

Tractor

Draw lines to label the parts of a tractor.

engine

wheel

exhaust

tyre

axle

steering wheel

cabin

Vehicles with a purpose

Look at each vehicle, and fill in the table for each one.

	Name of vehicle	What is it used for?	Number of axles	Number of wheels

Hands up!

How do these puppets work?

Cut out two shapes like this from material. Add eyes, ears, a nose and a mouth. Dress your puppet. What will you call it?

Wind-up action

These toys all use a wind-up mechanism. Label the parts.

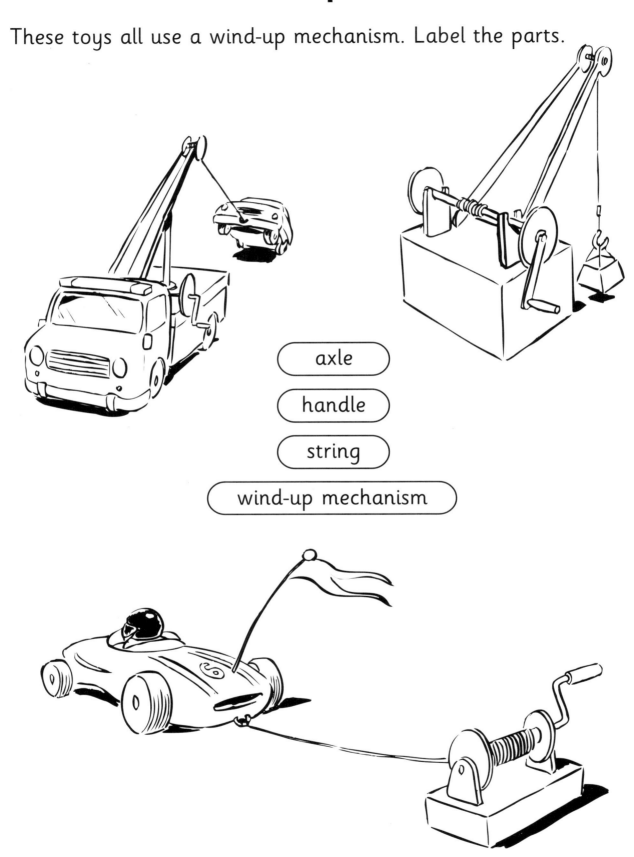

axle

handle

string

wind-up mechanism

Describe how these toys work.

Hickory Dickory Dock

Make the mouse run up the clock using a wind-up mechanism.

Things you might find useful:

masking tape

cotton reels

weights

dowel rods

string

card

scissors

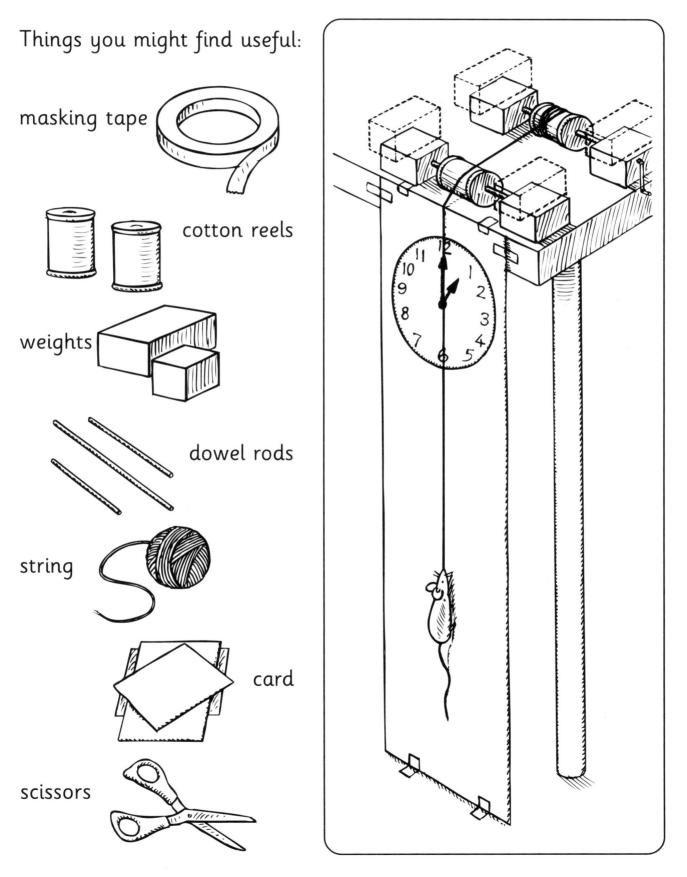

A fishy business

Try out different patterns for your fish.

ICT

Key Stage 1 is where children learn to use ICT confidently, becoming familiar with hardware and software, and using it to develop ideas and record creative work. The four aspects of study given in the National Curriculum are 'finding things out', 'developing ideas and making things happen', 'exchanging and sharing information' and 'reviewing, modifying and evaluating work as it progresses'. There is also a statutory requirement to use ICT across the curriculum. For Year 2 children, the QCA Scheme of Work provides five units to cover the curriculum, but with no estimate of the time required to complete all its demands satisfactorily. The following worksheets can be used as part of teaching to cover the work set out in the QCA ICT Scheme, Units 2A to 2E.

Most ICT work requires technology – after all, that is the point of the subject – but there are ways in which worksheets can support some of the ICT objectives in Year 2. For the most part these sheets underpin basic ideas (as with the 'A question of yes and no' sheets on pages 143 and 144), or provide stepping stones to work with particular hardware or software (as with 'Turtle turns to treasure' on page 142, and the ideas for creating pictures).

Bold key presses (page 139)

Objective: To learn that text can be entered and corrected on a computer (BACKSPACE, SPACE, SHIFT and RETURN keys).

What to do: This activity requires access to a computer, which children may need to do over a period of time if access is limited. Show the class some examples of word-processed text, and talk about how it might have been produced on the computer. Talk about its advantages and disadvantages (text is easy to correct, change, edit, but it is difficult to keep different versions of the text). Run through the processes described on the sheet, demonstrating them to the children if necessary. It is best if the children tackle one section of the sheet before moving onto the next. Make sure they recognise the highlighted keys on the drawing of the keyboard on the sheet.

Differentiation: If support is needed, let children work in pairs. More able children could try making other lists using the keys on the keyboard.

Extension: Give children a prepared text with a number of errors and omissions for the children to correct using what they have learned on the sheet

(use of spaces, capital letters, return key, backspace and so on).

Creating captions (page 140)

Objective: To develop the use of text on a screen.

What to do: Before tackling this activity, the children need to have practised the processes covered in the previous worksheet. Look at the picture on the sheet, and point out the caption to the children – can they think of anything else that could be written to match the story in the picture? Using a word processor, ask the children to write their own captions for the picture. This might be long or short, and need not include the caption given. Completed captions could be printed out and stuck underneath the picture, which could be coloured and suitably framed.

Differentiation: Look at more examples of picture captions to familiarise children with what's required: examine reading books and comics. Most children should recognise the story on the sheet (Little Red Riding Hood – of course), but tell the story to those who don't.

Extension: Give children opportunities to practise the techniques they have learned. Make sure it is a real task – real text written for an audience (perhaps a notice announcing the school Open Day, or a story for a younger child).

A burst of colour (page 141)

Objective: To learn that ICT can be used to make pictures.

What to do: Children need to have reasonable mouse control skills for this activity, and you will need appropriate graphics software on the classroom computer (*Microsoft Paint*, which comes free with Windows, is adequate if you have no other software available). Talk about the image on the sheet – you might like to ask the children to colour this in first. If the children have not been introduced to a graphics package, take them through using the particular tools illustrated on the worksheet. Can they make a design similar to the worksheet using the graphics package? Make sure they understand not to copy the picture on the sheet (one way to avoid this is to show a variety of pictures, for example by Mondrian and Matisse, to give them ideas).

Differentiation: Some children will need time to simply play with the program before attempting the challenge, although this activity is intended to focus this sort of experimentation. Children could work in pairs if necessary. Make sure that adult support is on hand to deal with the inevitable technical problems.

Extension: Follow-up work is included on the sheet: designing a 'freer' pattern such as Bonfire Night is excellent practice. Print the results and display them in the classroom.

Pirate Pete's Map

Turtle turns to treasure (page 142)

Objective: To understand that controlled devices can follow instructions.

What to do: The children should work in small groups on this assignment. The island can be built on a patio, on the playground, in a hall or other available space, using chairs, boxes and other equipment to create the obstacles shown on the map. Alternatively, you could simply mark the areas using labels. The children should plot a route for the turtle to follow from 'turtle beach' to the treasure (they can follow a route of their own devising, not necessarily the one on the map, although point out that the turtle would wish to avoid the obstacles!). They should record their routes using the shorthand suggested (for example, F25 for 'forward 25'), with the aim of presenting the route to another group to test. Can they make the turtle reach the treasure by following the instructions on the map?

Differentiation: The sheet assumes some basic familiarity with the idea of controlling a turtle with a set of instructions. Some children may need to be reminded about how to write these instructions. Plan out and create the island for less able children to use, so they can concentrate on writing the instructions. Provide adult support if needed.

Extension: Any reasonable programming challenge can be used for follow-up work. Can the children make the turtle 'walk' round the teacher's desk? Or perhaps make it find its way to the toilet?

A question of yes and no
(pages 143 and 144)

Objective: To develop simple 'yes/no' questioning techniques.

What to do: These two worksheets constitute one activity. Introduce the children to the creature from outer space on the first worksheet and explain the challenge: to devise a set of questions that will help the alien tell one vehicle from another. Explain that each question must only be answerable by a simple yes or no (so the result will be a paper-based binary tree). Although some instructions are included on the sheet, this exercise requires direct teaching in small groups.

Prepare by cutting out the pictures, arrows and question strips on the worksheets and mounting them on card. (The children can colour the 'yes' and 'no' arrows in black and red, as instructed.) Select two vehicles, say car and bus, and as a class devise a simple question that will distinguish the two (for example, 'Is it big?') Write the question on a question strip and place it on the desk. Underneath, place one 'no' and one 'yes' arrow pointing down in different directions; place the bus picture under the 'yes' arrow, and the car beneath the 'no' arrow. Select another picture, say the racing car. Ask the first question again: *Is it big?* It too will go beneath the 'no' arrow, where the car already resides. Now devise a question that will distinguish the car and the racing car: *Can it go very fast?* Put this question beneath the first 'no' arrow, place further 'yes' and 'no' arrows beneath it, and the racing car and normal car accordingly. Follow this procedure for each picture, returning to the first question each time a new picture is introduced, until all the vehicles are sorted. Don't worry – this is much more complicated to explain than to do! When complete, the groups will be able to follow the question tree and check the path of each vehicle to see how important asking the right question is.

Differentiation: Some children will need support with this activity, although the important part (asking appropriate questions), should not be beyond the capability of most of the class.

Extension: Add another vehicle (a van, petrol tanker, or minibus, for example). Can the children devise more questions to cope with this addition? They might make a record of their work by copying the completed binary tree onto a large sheet of paper. You can make further binary trees by using pictures or objects of another category (birds, fruit, sea creatures).

Bold key presses

Try these:

To rub out mistakes
Use the BACKSPACE key
to rub out any mistakes.

To make a capital letter
Hold down the SHIFT key as
you press a letter key.

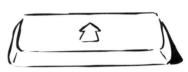

To put a space between words
Press the SPACE bar.

Try this:
Monday Tuesday Wednesday Thursday Friday Saturday Sunday

Can you make a vertical list?
Try making the days of
the week into a vertical
list.

Creating captions

Remember to use these keys on the keyboard:

This picture came from a story book. Which story is it?

_____

Type some more text that goes with the picture.
This is called a **caption**.

Hello Grandma. Are you feeling better?

A burst of colour

Use a drawing program to make your own brightly coloured pattern with shapes and lines like these.

Use the 'Fill' , 'Paintbrush' and 'Line'

tools to help you.

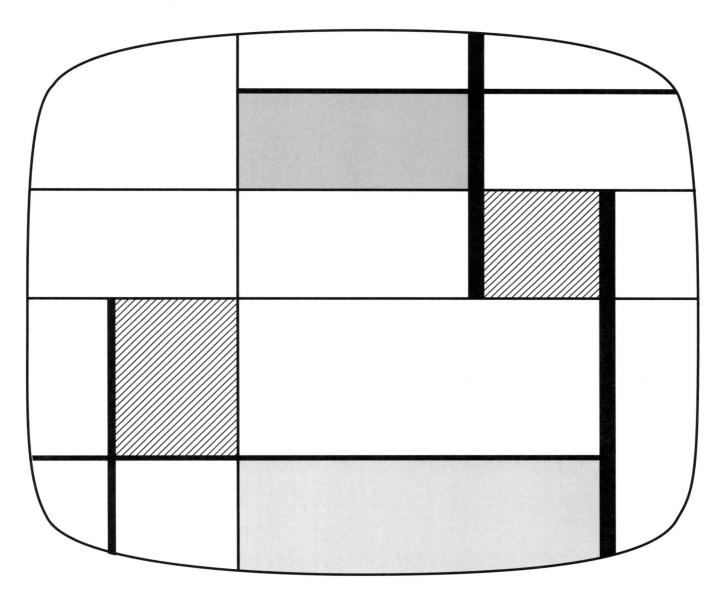

Try this:
Make a firework picture using the skills you have learned.

Turtle turns to treasure

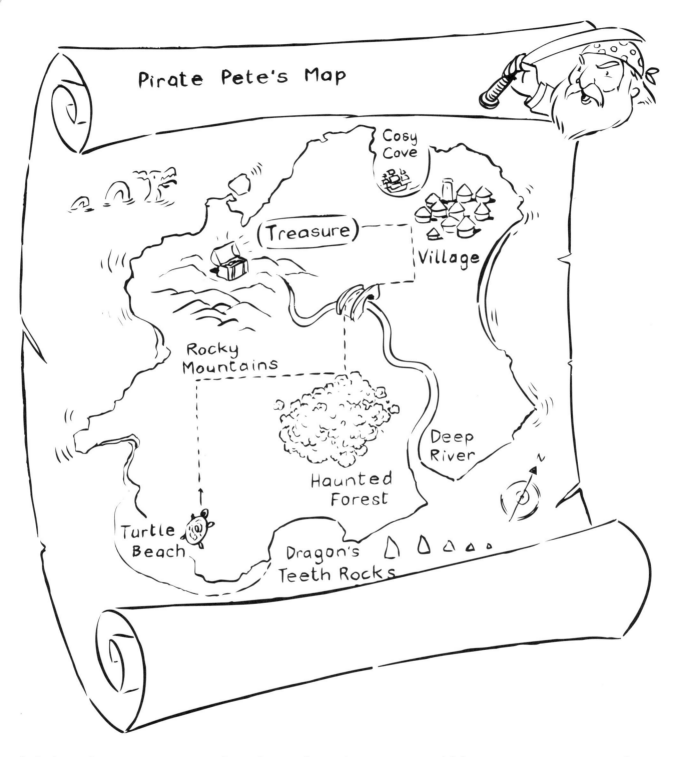

Make this treasure island in the classroom. Write instructions for the turtle to use so it can reach the treasure.

F = forward   L = left   R = right

A question of yes and no (1)

Cut out these pictures

A question of yes and no (2)

Colour and cut out these arrows:

Yes = black

No = red

Cut out five of each.
Cut out these question strips.

ART AND DESIGN

Children at Key Stage 1 are expected to 'explore the visual, tactile and sensory qualities of materials and processes and begin to understand and use colour, shape and space, and pattern and texture to represent their own ideas and feelings.' They are also required to examine and question the work of creative people – whether they are artists, designers, architects or sculptors. This latter aspect is the art equivalent of geographical fieldwork, and exposure to the work of creative people is one of the most important aspects of any programme of work for very young children.

In this section we have tried to focus on what worksheets can do, and have left the world of the tactile and sensory for you to introduce to the children. The QCA scheme allocates some 28–34 hours to art and design, but this subject is time-hungry, and you may well find that you wish to allocate more. These worksheets support some aspects of the QCA units 2A, 2B and 2C ('Picture this!', 'Mother Nature designer' and 'Can buildings speak?'), although they can, of course, be used independently of the units or be integrated with other comparable content if you are not following the QCA scheme.

Out of sight (page 147)

Objective: To visualise the whole of an image from a given part.

What to do: You might prefer to enlarge this worksheet to A3 size, although it can be used as it is. Talk to the children about the picture: *What might be 'out of sight'?* Talk about the visual clues in the picture – the lines, objects and so on. Ask the children first to colour in the given part of the picture (using whatever medium you choose), and then to continue the picture outwards until they have filled the rest of the frame. Encourage them to use their imagination to complete the task – remember there are no 'right' answers. Display and compare the work of a number of children when they have finished.

Differentiation: Less able children might work better on a larger copy of the worksheet. Give children who need more support and encouragement a fraction of a postcard, birthday card or Christmas card, then show how this fits into the complete picture to model the activity.

Extension: Extend this idea using old picture cards. In this case, use the same basic idea but introduce colour and colour matching into the activity. Stick the cards (or fractions of them) onto paper and ask children to paint or crayon an extension of the picture. Enlarge the worksheet if the children find the size too small and fiddly.

Which way round? (page 148)

Objective: To learn the difference between landscape and portrait orientation, and to be selective in the choice of a viewpoint.

What to do: Talk with the children about how a picture can be portrait (tall and thin) or landscape (short and fat), looking at examples if possible. Make sure that the children understand the instructions on the sheet (writing 'P' or 'L' by the side of the pictures is sufficient for this exercise). Explain that when they sketch their car race picture there is no right answer; it depends on what they choose to show in their picture and how it is framed.

Differentiation: Most schools have plenty of artwork on display. Take less confident children on an 'art gallery' tour of the school. Let them decide which pictures are landscape and which are portrait. Alternatively, provide them with picture cards (Christmas cards, postcards and so on) to sort into these categories. More able children could experiment with different framing options of the same picture to see which they think looks best.

Extension: Make picture frames (some children will be capable of making their own) – empty rectangles of card about the size of a computer disk which, when held at arm's length, frame a picture for a photograph or painting. Experiment with framing pictures in the classroom, and encourage children to choose between landscape and portrait for each 'shot'. If you have access to a camera, take a selection of the children's chosen pictures.

Design a pot (page 149)

Objective: To look at the design of everyday objects; to experiment with design, using first-hand observation for inspiration.

What to do: Unless preliminary work is undertaken this sheet will be a rather vacuous colouring-book exercise. The children must first look at and talk about different kinds of design they might see on everyday things (stick to pottery and crockery if you wish). Provide real examples for the children to examine in the classroom, and talk about how people who design these things might get ideas for their designs. Introduce a source or sources of ideas for their designs (perhaps nature). Look at the school grounds, flowers, trees, birds, insects, for inspiration. The children need not copy what they see, simply draw inspiration from it – long grass might suggest fine wavy lines, bees might suggest a black and yellow colour scheme. Display and compare the designs.

Differentiation: Encourage children to use simple line designs (for example, leaf shapes) or more complex designs according to their ability. Make sure that children have lots of time to discuss and think about what they are doing.

Extension: Ask children to observe and record shapes and colours in nature that they can find around them. Make a collection of non-living materials (a fallen branch, roots, leaves – don't encourage children to pick flowers) for a class display and provide magnifying glasses for children to examine them closely. Create a bank of words that describe textures, colours and shapes (shiny, gnarled, dotted, wrinkly, long and so on). A digital camera is also a useful tool for recording colours, textures and designs.

Window shapes (page 150)

Objective: To learn about the similarities and differences in buildings, identifying shapes and patterns.

What to do: Children should look at the pictures on the worksheet and use it as an 'I-spy' sheet, ticking off the windows they have seen. This activity should ideally follow a local walk; you might even use it as part of a field study. Ask the children to describe each window (this could be done orally, or by a word or short phrase written on the sheet). From first-hand experience, ask the children to draw and describe another window of their choice.

Differentiation: If necessary, ask less able children to concentrate only on windows that can be seen in and around the school.

Extension: There are many other aspects of buildings that might form the focus for further work. You might,

for example, make rubbings of textures and shapes on the school building, or record the patterns of bricks on walls. Alternatively, ask children to make a brief guide to the chimneys (or a similar focus) of the locality.

Patterns in doors (page 151)

Objective: To learn about the similarities and differences in buildings, identifying shapes and patterns.

What to do: This sheet complements work on the previous sheet, and should be used in a similar way. As a follow-up to a project on buildings, ask the children to discuss what they think about the things they have studied and drawn. Ask: *What do you think and feel about these buildings? What about the work you have produced?* (This will help to meet the requirement to evaluate and develop work.)

Out of sight

What might be in the rest of this picture? Draw what you think.

Which way round?

This is a portrait picture

This is a landscape picture

Look at these pictures. Write **P** by pictures that are portrait and **L** by pictures that are landscape.

Which frame would you choose for a picture of a car race? Draw your picture here.

Design a pot

Write one word that each design makes you think of under each teapot.

Make your own design for this teapot.

Window shapes

Talk about these windows. Can you see any like these?

Draw and describe a different window of your own choice.

Patterns in doors

Talk about these doors. Can you see any like these?

Draw and describe a different door of your own choice.

MUSIC

The National Curriculum for music states that 'By the end of Year 2, most children will be able to recognise and explore how sounds are organised.' Part of this will involve exercising ears, voice and performing skills (singing with a sense of shape and melody, for example). These are activities in which paper resources can only play a small part because the curriculum places emphasis on experience. Knowledge and understanding of music will come through an active curriculum of performing, composing and appraising. But although the curriculum requires children to learn to control sounds through singing and playing (performing), to create and develop musical ideas (composing), and to make improvements to their own work (appraising), there are nevertheless aspects of this that worksheets can support.

All music work in Year 2 should be set in the context of musical experience, whether that be listening or performing. When listening, we must put in a plea that the best possible instruments and electronic methods of sound reproduction be used. Children should be given the best because, by and large, they will be used to the best in the cinema, on TV and with CDs, where the quality of modern sound reproduction, even on relatively cheap systems, is excellent. If your school cannot meet modern standards then a new sound system should go to the top of your shopping list!

Feeling the pulse (page 154)

Objective: To identify the beat in music.

What to do: An adult will need to provide the children with a lead in this work. Practise clapping the rhythm of nursery rhymes together, and play music with a strong, easily identifiable pulse to the children, clapping the rhythm as you go. Use music with contrasting speeds to demonstrate the idea to the children. Clap the rhythms given on the sheet, then let the children work in pairs to practise clapping the pulses before working out a pulse for a nursery rhyme such as 'Here we go round the mulberry bush'.

Differentiation: Some children might need to tackle this work in a small group with adult support. Children may find it easier to tap out the pulse on their knees rather than clapping.

Extension: Introduce the children to a variety of tempos. Have fun singing and clapping to a variety of songs, noticing how speed can change the mood of a piece. For example, you could try singing a lullaby quickly, or singing a fast, cheerful song ponderously slowly – the songs sound entirely different. An electronic keyboard is a good instrument for demonstrating different beats in music.

Copy claps (page 155)

Objective: To recall and copy rhythmic patterns.

What to do: A tambourine, tambour or drum is required for this lesson. As a class (or in small groups), tap out a four-beat rhythm – the children can take it in turns to tap this out on a tambourine.

Keep the rhythm going, and tap out the patterns of names such as teacher's names, famous people, the months of the year, the name of the school or local streets, making them fit in with the four beats. The children should echo this pattern. Ask the children to write out their name and clap its rhythm (an adult needs to listen to check that they can fit the name to the pulse). Play the game suggested on the worksheet in small groups. Note that the patterns clapped may be on the beat, last more than a beat or be faster than the beat.

Differentiation: Plenty of practice and lots of experience of listening to music is the way in which to build up awareness of pulse and rhythm – for those who find this difficult there is no substitute for experience. Children lacking the foundation of singing nursery rhymes will be at a disadvantage here, so you will need to provide experiences to compensate for this. Daily repetition and work in supportive groups is recommended.

Extension: Once the children can beat out rhythmic patterns of words, the next step is to beat out a rhythmic pattern without reference to a word pattern. Can the children make up a pattern to play on an untuned percussion instrument that will fit with your four-beat pulse? (This a challenge that can only be met after a great deal of practice.)

A dotty game (page 156)

Objective: To play and sing phrases from dot notation.

What to do: Provide glockenspiels or chime bars and beaters, giving different children a note each from the sheet. Although the children can simply follow the instructions on the sheet, it would be better if the note cards were cut out and mounted. Provide a few blank cards for the children to compose their own tunes on. Place the cards on a music stand (or similar) in order to make playing and reading easier – the children should be able to find the starting note from the position of the dots on the cards (the higher the dot is on the card, the higher the pitch – as in musical notation). Encourage the use of both beaters.

Differentiation: Allow less able children to use just one beater initially. Make sure that only the notes chosen are provided not the full scale – separate chime bars are best for this.

Extension: Challenge the children to make a five-note tune, using just the three notes that they have. Remind them that they can have silences (rests), repeated notes and some notes played for longer than others. The latter might be shown by the spacing of the dots – closer together for faster, more widely spaced for longer notes. The names of the notes can be written under the dots if required.

Making instruments make sound (page 157)

Objective: To identify different ways instruments make sound; to perform together using different types of instruments.

What to do: You will need to give the children access to a range of classroom instruments for this activity – a 'music corner' is an ideal solution. Explain the activity to the children – that they should colour-code the instruments according to how they are played as they complete the sheet.

Once they have completed this part of the activity, cut the labels at the top of the sheet out (enlarged and mounted on card is best) and give them to one child, who acts as conductor. Give five children (or groups) an instrument or instruments that match to one or more of the categories. When the conductor holds up a card, that group of instruments should play for as long as the card is displayed. The conductor can vary the choice of cards and the amount of time they are displayed for to create a 'performance'.

Differentiation: You may need to demonstrate the available instruments to show the children how they can be played.

Extension: Challenge children to find a way of writing down the 'performance' that they have created. Can they find a way of marking the duration and volume of the sound required? You might like to arrange a visit that will give children experience of musicians playing a range of instruments.

Sound resources (1) and (2)
(pages 158 and 159)

Objective: To show how symbols can be used for changing sounds.

What to do: The cards on this and the next worksheet can be used with groups of children playing instruments to see how they can alter the sound that their instrument makes. Talk about what the pictures on the worksheets show, and what kind of sound they represent. Ask the children to colour the cards as directed on the sheet, then cut them out and mount them so they can be re-used. One child should act as conductor to the group, holding up one card at a time to direct the children's playing. As this develops, the conductor could hold up two different cards at a time, so the children should play, for example, low and slow.

Differentiation: Ask an adult to check that the children can interpret the symbols correctly. You may want to limit the game to displaying one card only for groups of less able children. It may also be helpful to enlarge the cards on the sheet so they can be seen more easily.

Extension: Give a group of children a scene to describe under the direction of their conductor (a walk through a dark wood, creeping through a haunted school, a bicycle journey over a mountain) using music appropriate to the scene. Can they find a way of writing down their composition?

Sound story (page 160)

Objective: To learn how words can describe sounds and how sounds can describe scenes.

What to do: Look at the weather with the class. Talk about the different kinds of sound that the weather can make, and think of some words that we might use to describe it. Look at the first picture on the sheet and explain the instructions to the children (you might read the words given in a voice to match the words; the children will enjoy doing this themselves). For the second part of the sheet, ask the children to choose instruments that match the weather conditions described, before moving on to tell the story, using sound, of the calm after the storm (starting, of course, with the storm itself).

Differentiation: For less able children, provide cards with lots of descriptive words written on them, and ask them to choose words that might fit each picture.

Extension: Each day, choose a different group of children to describe the weather using instruments. They should explain their choices to the class.

Feeling the pulse

✖   ✖   ✖   ✖
Half a pound of tuppenny rice

✖   ✖   ✖ ✖
Half a pound of treacle

✖   ✖   ✖   ✖
That's the way the money goes

✖ ✖   ✖ ✖
POP goes the weasel!

Say the rhyme, and clap the pulses marked ✖.

●   ●
Half a pound of tuppenny rice

●   ●
Half a pound of treacle

●   ●
That's the way the money goes

●   ●
POP goes the weasel!

Say the rhyme again, clapping where the ● s are.
Which is the quicker pulse – the first rhyme or the second rhyme?

Sing and clap the pulse to this song. Mark the words you clap on.

Here we go round the mulberry bush,

The mulberry bush, the mulberry bush.

Here we go round the mulberry bush,

On a cold and frosty morning.

Copy claps

Clap this strong pulse.

Tap the pulse on a tambourine.

Write your name here _____

Clap out its rhythm.

Clap out the name of your favourite TV programme. Can your friend guess what it is?

A dotty game

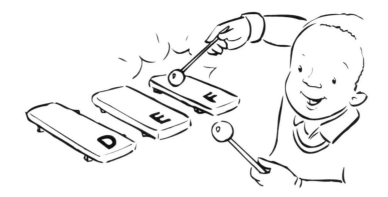

Take these three notes and two beaters. Play these tunes using the notes.

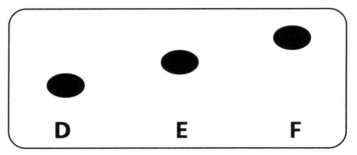

Sing them to **la**.

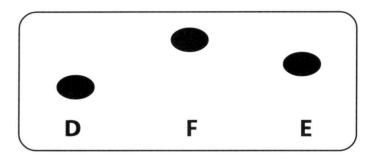

Can you make up your own tunes with these notes? Write it down.

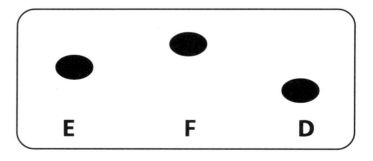

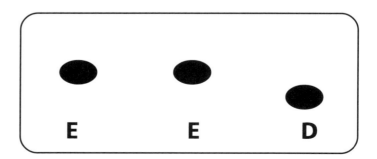

Making instruments make sound

| Tapping |  Scraping |  Shaking |  Blowing | 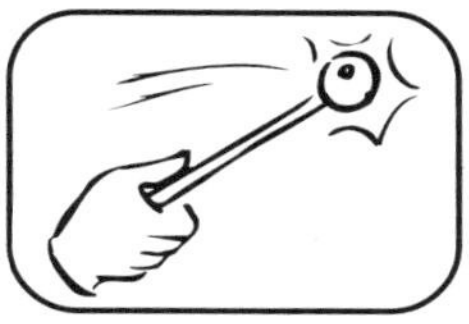 Striking |

Colour the pictures in lightly.

Take one instrument to match each card.

Find out their names and write them down. Draw a picture of each instrument.

Tapping _____

Shaking _____

Scraping _____

Blowing _____

Striking _____

Sound resources (1) Pitch and dynamics

low

high

loud

quiet

Colour the cards and cut them out so you can conduct your orchestra.

Sound resources (2) Duration and tempo

long

short

fast

slow

Colour the cards and cut them out so you can conduct your orchestra.

Sound story

What sound words might describe this picture? Make a list.

thunder	howling	
rumbling		
pitter patter		

Choose some instruments to make these sounds.

What sound words might describe this picture? Make a list.

Use instruments to tell a story from the first picture to the second.

RELIGIOUS EDUCATION

In some ways, RE is the 'odd one out' in the school curriculum – it is certainly at times the subject of controversy, so it is worth restating what its status is. Although there are 12 National Curriculum subjects (including citizenship at Key Stages 3 and 4), religious education is not one of them. RE is, however, a statutory requirement and must be taught according to a locally agreed syllabus in all maintained schools (except voluntary aided schools and schools of a religious character, where religion should be taught according to a trust deed or guidelines).

Agreed syllabuses tend to tread the same ground, sharing common elements, and the QCA have felt confident enough to produce a Scheme of Work, even though there is no 'national' curriculum around which it might fit. Because religion is closely bound up in strongly held beliefs, faith communities and cultural heritage, the syllabuses that emerge from QCA and local SACREs, can sometimes sit uneasily with children's levels of maturity. In their formulation they have to satisfy many demands, expectations and pressures.

We have tried to support the main thrusts of the QCA scheme in this section. For Year 2 the scheme proposes four study units (two less than Year 1), with an indicated teaching time of 24 hours in total. Two study units are generic (dealing with celebrations and visiting places of worship), and two are specific (the Torah and the stories of Jesus). The scheme emphasises that not only is there no compulsion to use it, but that schools might opt to 'pick and choose' material from it in order to meet the demands of the locally agreed syllabus. Treat these worksheets in the same way: ignore those that do not apply, and amend those that do not quite fit the needs of your school. Where questions about a particular faith community are involved rather than general information, advice is best sought from the faith community itself.

The Torah: A holy book (page 163)

Objective: To learn about the Torah and how it is treated by Jews as a holy book.

What to do: This sheet should follow preliminary work on Judaism, and should not be used 'cold'. Work with a small group, reading through the sheet with the children. Discuss what we mean when we say something is 'holy'. The children should be able to tackle the latter part of the sheet unaided, after a little discussion: *Are there any things at home, at Grandma's, at your friend's house, that you are not allowed to touch?*

Note that the Torah (Torah means teaching) is only part of the Jewish holy book; it should not be referred to as the Jewish Bible. The Torah was given to Moses on Mount Sinai and is also known as the oral law. It is the first five books of the Bible.

Differentiation: Give penty of adult support and encouragement. Do any of the children possess a special toy, photograph or item of clothing? Ask: *Why is it special? How do you treat it differently from other things that you possess?*

Extension: Ask children to make a list of rules for respecting things that are precious to other people, for example 'Don't touch without permission', 'Handle with care', 'Don't make fun of things that are special to other people'.

Rules for living (page 164)

Objective: To reflect on words from the Torah that give guidance for living; to consider rules for living.

What to do: Talk about 'rules for living', and make a class list of the children's ideas (carrying shopping, running errands, giving up a seat on a bus, speaking respectfully, taking care not to crash into elderly people in rough play and so on). Ask: *How would we carry out these rules in practice?* Ask the children to draw an illustration of the rule on the worksheet, and to compile their 'three rules for living' based on the class discussion.

Differentiation: Help children to talk about why we should treat old people with respect. Use old people known to them as examples.

Extension: Choose another rule from the Torah (for example, Leviticus 19:18: 'Love your neighbour as you love yourself') and talk with the children about how they could put this into practice.

A story told by Jesus: The prodigal son (page 165)

Objective: To learn that Jesus told stories, and that these stories were a way of teaching people about God, how to behave and treat each other.

What to do: Read the story on the worksheet aloud to the children (the story appears in Luke 15). Stop occasionally and ask: *How do you think X felt? What do you think Y might have said then?* The children should follow the cartoon story and add speech of their own in the spaces on the worksheet.

Differentiation: Some children will need reminding of the story and may not be able to read the captions, so some reading support should be given. This could be made into a co-operative exercise, in mixed-ability groups.

Extension: Talk about what the parable teaches with the children. Do they think that the father treated both sons well? Ask the children to learn another story told by Jesus, and to retell it to the class. You could make a class 'storyboard' of another parable.

A story told by Jesus: Firm foundations (page 166)

Objective: To learn that Jesus told stories and that these stories were a way of teaching people about God, how to behave and treat each other.

What to do: This story can be told (and indeed sung!) with the children. Explain that it was a story told by Jesus. Ask questions as the story is told: *What was Jesus thinking? What might he have said?* The children should complete the speech balloons appropriately (they need not be long sentences: 'Help!' might be apposite in one of the balloons!).

Differentiation: Adult support for the writing part may be necessary.

Extension: Ask groups of children to act out the story. Talk about what we can learn from this story with the children.

Religious celebrations (page 167)

Objective: To understand that religious festivals are a special type of celebration.

What to do: This is an impossible sheet to tackle unless the children have been introduced to, or have experience of, at least two of the festivals illustrated. Treat the pictures as a description exercise only. Let the children talk about the pictures, extract what information they can from them, and speculate about what is happening (they do not have to know the 'right' answers). The second part of the challenge is for the children to write something about two of the festivals on the sheet. Provide reference materials and support for this part of the activity. The exercise must be set in the context of a class project to find out about other cultures and religions, so focus children's attention on the religious aspects of the festivals.

Differentiation: This is a difficult exercise, and some children may need adult support to complete the sheet. It would help if you can provide plenty of visual material, reference books and even videos to aid the children.

Extension: Focus on one of the festivals, and look more closely to give children a greater insight into its practice and meaning. Ideally, ask someone from the faith community in question to come and talk to the children about the festival. You might like to focus on one aspect of the festival, such as special foods, dress or ceremonies.

Visiting places of worship (page 168)

Objective: To learn that religious communities have special expectations about how people should behave when they visit their place of worship.

What to do: Make sure the children understand the instructions on the sheet before they complete it. It is best if this exercise is carried out in small mixed-ability groups. When the children have finished, compare the rules from each group. Are there any rules common to everyone?

Differentiation: The support of working in a group should be sufficient for most children.

Extension: Visit a nearby place of worship. This should be done by special arrangement, ideally with a guide. Check on the rules for visitors and explain them to children before you go. Ask the children to compile a code of conduct based upon their work on this sheet.

The Torah: A holy book

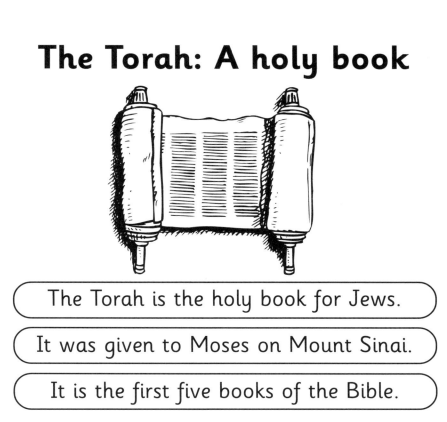

The Torah is the holy book for Jews.

It was given to Moses on Mount Sinai.

It is the first five books of the Bible.

A Torah scroll is **holy** to the Jews. It is treated as very special.

The writing is not touched.

It is lifted up and shown to people.

Jews stand up and bow their heads.

Are there special things at home that you are forbidden to touch? Why?

Draw a picture of something that is special to you.
Why is it special?

Rules for living

The Jewish holy book, the Torah, contains rules for living.
This is one of the rules:

> "Show respect for old people and honour them."

How might you obey this?
Draw a picture and write a caption underneath.

Make up three more good rules for living.

_____

_____

_____

A story told by Jesus: The prodigal son

This is a story told by Jesus. Complete the speech bubbles.

A man had two sons. He gave half his land to each.

The younger son sold his land and went off to spend all his money.

He had no money and had to mind pigs. He was starving.

He was so hungry, he went home. His father was delighted to see him and made a special feast to celebrate.

When the older son came home from working in the fields, he was angry. "I work hard but you don't give me a feast."

His father told him that he was always at home, and he gave him everything. His brother had come home and they should celebrate.

A story told by Jesus: Firm foundations

The wise man...

chose a good rocky place to build a house...

the rains came down...

the house stood firm.

The foolish man...

found a sandy place that looked nice...

the flood came up...

the house fell down.

Religious celebrations

Religious festivals are a special kind of celebration. What is happening in these pictures? Write a sentence about two of these festivals.

Christmas

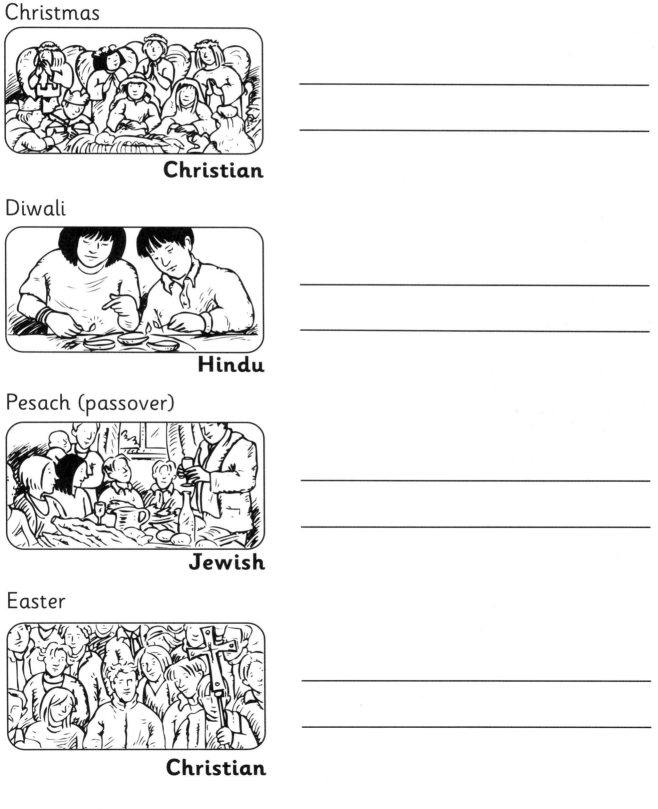

Christian

_____

_____

Diwali

Hindu

_____

_____

Pesach (passover)

Jewish

_____

_____

Easter

Christian

_____

_____

Visiting places of worship

Do you have rules in your home?

Take off outdoor shoes.

Keep your bedroom tidy.

Wash your hands before meals.

Dirty clothes go in the washing basket.

Finish this sentence:

In my house you must: _____

_____

_____

Churches and other places of worship are special places and must be treated with respect. Make up some rules for a school visit.

Rules

_____

_____

_____

_____

_____

_____

PSHE AND CITIZENSHIP

PSHE and citizenship are not National Curriculum subjects at Key Stage 1 (although citizenship is a statutory requirement at Key Stages 3 and 4). Schools are, nevertheless, expected to promote spiritual, moral, social and cultural development across the National Curriculum at all key stages. To this end, the government has provided a non-statutory framework for PSHE and citizenship at Key Stages 1 and 2.

The knowledge, skills and understanding required are to be taught under the following headings: 'Developing confidence and responsibility and making the most of their abilities', 'Preparing to play an active role as citizens', 'Developing a healthy, safer lifestyle' and 'Developing good relationships and respecting differences between people'. But because of the non-statutory nature of this framework and the lack of content prescription, there are many ways of teaching to these headings – we can only scratch the surface of the subject here. The Calouste Gulbenkian Foundation has, for example, produced what amounts to a scheme of work for the subject (*Passport: A framework for personal and social development*), which has been sent to every school in the country. But we have tried to make sure that these photocopiable sheets can be used to support any approach to the subject that tries to work within the National Curriculum framework.

Meet the needs
(page 171)

Objective: To understand that people, animals and plants have needs.

What to do: This activity is simple. The children should examine the pictures on the left of the page, then draw (or write) what they think is needed in the picture in the blank frame provided. For example, the cat is hungry, so they would need to provide a saucer of milk; the plant needs watering, so it should be watered.

Differentiation: Less confident children could tackle this activity in a group, with adult support if necessary to direct the discussion. Pictures rather than words are acceptable from less able children.

Extension: This worksheet intends to underpin the understanding that everyone has similar basic needs, so you might follow this up by discussing what these needs might be. Ask children to write down one or two needs they think that everybody shares. This could be a homework task.

Needs and wants (page 172)

Objective: To understand that there is a difference between wants and needs.

What to do: Make sure that the children understand the instructions on the worksheet. They are fairly straightforward. The beginning of each sentence is missing, so the children need to complete the sentence by adding 'I want' or 'I need' to the start of it as they think appropriate. The answers are obvious to an adult, but you may need to discuss the possible answers with the children as they work through the sheet. The sentences at the end are left blank for the children's own ideas.

Differentiation: This is a literary sheet and should be read correctly, for which adult or group help may be needed to support less confident readers. All children should be able to cope with the writing, although some may need help with the last task.

Extension: Play a class or group game: in turn, each child has to say a sentence starting alternately with 'I want' or 'I need'. Any child who uses want or need incorrectly, or who cannot think of an answer, is 'out'. Continue until you have a winner (or winners) if you wish.

Saying 'no' (page 173)

Objective: To understand that they can say 'no' when something feels wrong.

What to do: Explain the worksheet to the children. Individually, or in a small group, they should examine each situation pictured and decide whether Ted should reply with a 'yes' or a 'no', writing the word in the empty speech balloon. The answers are obvious to an adult, but there needs to be some discussion after the sheet has been completed. Why have they given these answers? Adults, but not children, will pick up on the fact that it is possible to give a valid and sensible response in either way to some of the questions (the ride in the car is with Daddy, or Ted is sick so cannot go to the party, for example). Draw out the learning from the discussion: stranger danger, cruelty to animals and so on.

Differentiation: This should be a group task for less able children with, if necessary, an adult to assist.

Extension: You must make a judgement about the

direction you wish to take with this topic. It will depend on the curriculum that you are following – and timing is also important – but sensitive issues such as theft, child abuse (knowing that they have rights over their own bodies) and stranger danger may be appropriate follow-up work. Ask the children to think of other situations where 'no' would be the correct response, setting parameters for, say, things said in the playground, in a shop or in the park.

Red means danger (page 174)

Objective: To understand that there are rules for keeping safe at home and in the street.

What to do: The children will need red, yellow and green crayons or pencils for this activity, and they will need to be able to discriminate between these colours. Talk about the colours of the traffic lights, and how to match these colours to each of the pictures on the worksheet. Get the children to colour in the free lights at the top first. Explain the activity to the children. They should examine each situation pictured, and decide whether it is safe, if it requires care, or if it is clearly dangerous. There are a number of possible variations for answers to some of the questions, which could form the basis of a discussion, but the recommended responses are: water (red), crossing the road (yellow), drugs (red), electric fire (yellow), bread knife (red), boiling a kettle (red). Note that green has not been used, although the children may choose to do so. If this happens, talk about the responses with the children (why do they think it is safe to eat pills? Cut bread?) The answers are based on the assumption that children of this age should not do

certain things, even when supervised (such as cutting bread).

Differentiation: Group support is a sensible way of eliciting the best responses from less able children. Mixed-ability groups are best.

Extension: Get children to draw up lists of 'red' and 'yellow' situations. This is probably best done as a class exercise.

People who help us (1) and (2)
(pages 175 and 176)

Objective: To know about the people in the world and their function.

What to do: Two worksheets tackle this theme, and can be used individually or collectively. The aim is for the children to identify people who help us, but also to understand that there are adults who we can approach to ask for help in certain situations. There is also an underlying aim to teach children respect for all people regardless of job, colour, gender and so on. To complete the sheets the children should examine the people pictured on them, and fill in the blanks by responding to the questions asked. Follow-up discussion can be used to draw out and underline the aims of the sheets, and to make links to ideas such as 'stranger danger'.

Differentiation: Provide labels with the names of the jobs shown on the worksheets, and let less able children match the labels to the correct people. For those who are having difficulty with the writing, you could accept oral responses.

Extension: Display the answers as a gallery of 'people who help us'. Ask children to add another person to the display, following the pattern on the sheets. This could be a homework task.

Meet the needs

What is needed here? Draw or write what is needed in the spaces.

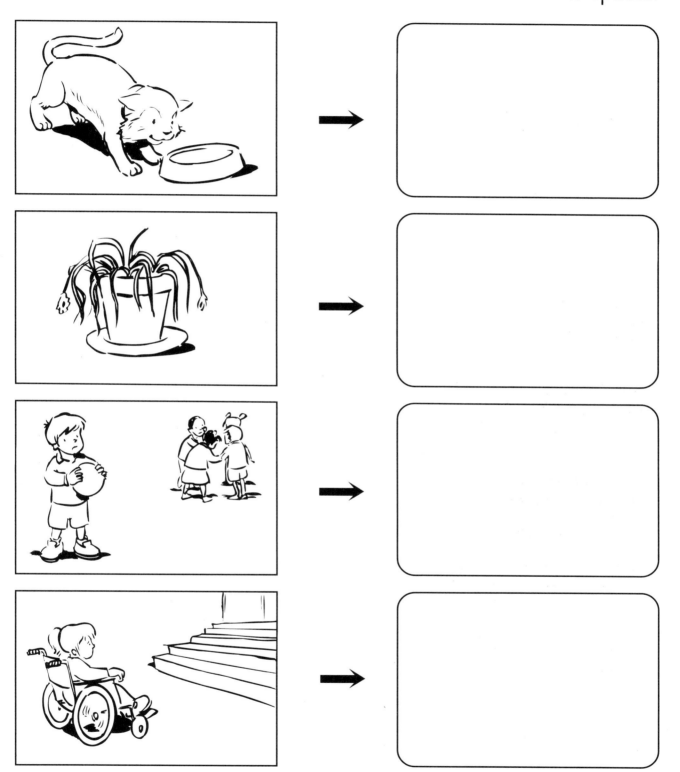

We all have needs. Write down one of your needs.

■ SCHOLASTIC   **171**

Needs and wants

Write "I want" or "I need" in the spaces.

_____ a big ice cream with chocolate.

_____ clothes to keep me warm.

_____ to meet Robbie Williams.

_____ a very fast car.

_____ to eat and drink regularly.

_____ a computer for Christmas.

Complete these sentences yourself.

I need _____

I want _____

Saying no

Ted is not sure when to say "yes" and when to say "no". Can you help? What should he say to each of these?

Explain your answers.

Red means danger

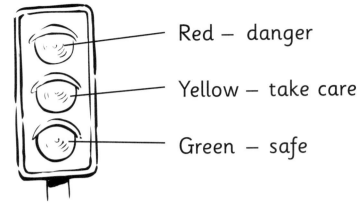

Red – danger

Yellow – take care

Green – safe

Colour the traffic lights

People who help us (1)

Who is this? _____

How does she help us? _____

_____

_____

Who is this? _____

How does he help us? _____

_____

_____

Who is this? _____

How does he help us? _____

_____

_____

Who is this? _____

How does she help us? _____

_____

_____

People who help us (2)

Who is this? _____

How does she help us? _____

_____

_____

Who is this? _____

How does he help us? _____

_____

_____

Who is this? _____

How does he help us? _____

_____

_____

Who is this? _____

How does he help us? _____

_____

_____